Praise for *Workshop Culture*

Workshop Culture offers a compelling rationale for why the culture created in a well-designed and led workshop is indeed a match for the kind of culture organizations engaged in knowledge work need to succeed. In author Alison Coward's telling, a workshop is no longer a time out, away from the real work; it is a *time in* – a time to focus deeply and collaboratively on what to do and how to do it well. Well-researched and beautifully written, this practical guidebook can be put to immediate use to help leaders build a thriving, engaged workforce.

Amy C. Edmondson, Novartis Professor of Leadership, Harvard Business School, author of *Right Kind of Wrong: The science of failing well*

Great workshops temporarily transform how we work. Alison Coward shows us how to make the transformation permanent. A smart guide to smart teamwork!

Jake Knapp, *New York Times* bestselling author of *Sprint*

Alison Coward's advocacy of work culture is compelling – who among us wouldn't prefer a work environment that's responsive, welcoming, safe and bursting with creative potential? She makes this possibility feel approachable and real. As a facilitator and collaboration designer, this book makes me want to applaud.

Sunni Brown, social entrepreneur and bestselling author

An engaging, practical, step-by-step guide for building a healthy, creative, inclusive and innovative workplace.

Dave Gray, co-author of *Gamestorming: A playbook for innovators, rulebreakers, and changemakers*

T0035220

At a time in which work is increasingly uncertain, employees are seeking more meaning and businesses are striving to maintain competitive advantage. This poignant and practical book is the go-to manual for leaders and teams looking to build a better culture. One of the sharpest and most experienced leaders in the field, Alison Coward's approach offers a robust, unique and above all actionable roadmap to help teams (and the organisations they work for) flourish and thrive. Drawing upon her deep expertise as a skilled and trusted facilitator, Alison guides the reader through the practices, principles and tools they'll need to transform their teams, attract and retain more talent and cultivate greater resilience, whatever their industry.

Nathalie Nahai, best-selling author of *Business Unusual*

As an invaluable tool for teams to learn, strategize, align and share, workshops have never been more important. Alison has a huge amount of experience in team dynamics and on advising how to get exceptional value from workshops. This book distills her essential insights into a very engaging and practical read to help teams transform how they work.

Neil Perkin, author of *Building the Agile Business* and
Agile Transformation

I've always been obsessed about culture, collaboration and the creation of high performing teams after founding The Social Element, a remote-first agency, back in 2002. We have worked with Alison; her approach outlined in this book enabled us to have an ongoing *Workshop Culture* at The Social Element, which has helped the team release their creativity, build trust and inspire each other and our clients every day.

Tamara Littleton, founder and CEO of The Social Element

Alison is rare in that she is a natural-born facilitator and has cultivated the skill of building highly effective teams for decades now. This is her playbook for all of us to indulge in. Deconstructing the principles that make for great workshops, Alison guides us to integrate these practices into our everyday working lives. If you want to gain the energy, motivation and positivity that comes from collaborative workshops – this is the book you need.

Jonas Altman, author of *Shapers: Reinvent the way you work and change the future*

Alison is one of the best communicators we have on the challenge of teams and making teams better.

This book is for everyone who wants their team to be more innovative, more creative, more change-ready – and more productive. As Alison says, 'workshops provide a snapshot into what a high-performing, engaged and collaborative team looks like' – and this readable, knowledgeable and above all actionable book brilliantly shows how to take the intense learning and agile thinking of a workshop into your team full-time, with frameworks, advice and a whole world of insight.

Richard Goff, Chair of The People Director Partnership

I founded Groove to bring people together and so I'm well aware that as the world of work evolves, we have more need for staying connected and finding ways of relating to each other. In *Workshop Culture*, Alison provides a persuasive argument for better collaboration and a practical framework for how we can find connection, self-awareness and balance in the workplace.

Josh Greene, co-founder and CEO of Groove

WORKSHOP CULTURE

A GUIDE TO BUILDING TEAMS THAT THRIVE

ALISON COWARD

First published in Great Britain by Practical Inspiration Publishing, 2024

© Alison Coward, 2024

The moral rights of the author have been asserted.

ISBN   9781788604710   (print)
          9781788604734   (epub)
          9781788604727   (mobi)

All rights reserved. This book, or any portion thereof, may not be reproduced without the express written permission of the author.

Front cover design: Gabija Jankauskaite
Author photo: Polly for Hey Tuesday

Every effort has been made to trace copyright holders and to obtain their permission for the use of copyright material. The publisher apologizes for any errors or omissions and would be grateful if notified of any corrections that should be incorporated in future reprints or editions of this book.

Want to bulk-buy copies of this book for your team and colleagues? We can customize the content and co-brand *Workshop Culture* to suit your business's needs.

Please email info@practicalinspiration.com for more details.

Practical Inspiration
Publishing

Contents

Foreword

I first met Alison Coward in 2012 at a conference in London, when our work around innovation was just taking off. Little would I know that Alison and I would develop a deep friendship and that she would go on to become a leading expert on workshops and facilitation.

The work that I focused on over the last two-plus decades was naturally centred around workshops. All the business tools that I helped develop play a crucial role in workshops. In fact, the Business Model Canvas came out of an effort to design a workshop on business models. Back when I was co-owner of a consultancy called Arvetica, I was preparing a workshop. I designed it based on the Business Model Ontology from my PhD work. Yet that was a classic conceptual model with rectangles and arrows; it was not workshop ready. It's when I drew lines between the rectangles that it became the Canvas, a workshop tool. Now workshop participants had a space to put up sticky notes. With that visual tool in hand, we were ready to run a workshop with a group of people from different backgrounds. The Canvas created a shared language for participants from different parts of the business to co-create a business model.

From there onwards I became fascinated by designing and running workshops. It helped me realize how powerful they were. Innovation teams, the audience I work with, can't function without them. Of course, my own very first workshops were terrible, and I only learned over time by trial and error how to perfect them. Luckily, you can use Alison's book to avoid the painful learning process I had to go through. This book is your shortcut to rolling out a workshop culture in the organizations you work for.

At Strategyzer, my company, workshops are an integral part of our company culture. They're everywhere; we use workshops all the time. It's made our work more engaging, clearer, more transparent, and more effective. We use them to better understand, iterate, align, and create buy-in. A great example of how we use workshops at Strategyzer are the company calls that we host every two months. We spend quite some time designing them. As a response to the COVID-19 pandemic, we designed a workshop to better understand everybody's concerns. To unleash better feedback, we designed a workshop to co-create potential actions. To improve collaboration, we designed a workshop to iterate a so-called Team Contract, which set the rules for which behaviours were 'in' and which ones were 'out'. (We prototyped this workshop in advance, since co-creating with large groups is not ideal.) To align on strategy, we designed a workshop around our Objectives and Key Results (OKRs). Most importantly, we avoid using any of these workshops for information-sharing purposes. Since we are a fully remote global company, synchronous time is very expensive. We share information in short pre-recorded video presentations in advance, and then fully dedicate the workshop to real work. We want *work*-shops, not *talk*-shops.

To write this foreword I reflected on my own learning journey when it comes to workshop design and facilitation, and how it has transformed me as a leader. There are three things that help me run great workshops. First, I spend an enormous amount of time preparing the workshop. I iterate and re-iterate the workshop flow until I believe it will help us reach the desired outcome. I also time the workshop down to the minute and consider energy management. A well-designed workshop is half the work done.

Second, I search for the right visual tools to make workshop activities tangible. In the workshops I'm involved in, there's often a visual artifact at the centre of the action. This could be an established visual tool like the Business Model Canvas, a Service Blueprint, or a Strategy Canvas. It could also be something as simple as a set of sticky notes to force-rank items. For example, you can use this technique to understand customer priorities. I also reflect on the right visual facilitation tools like Edward de Bono's Thinking Hats. They help you gather better and quicker feedback than a free-flow discussion ever could.

Third, over the years I learned how to hone my own facilitation skills. Most importantly, I realized that facilitation becomes easy with a strong workshop design. That's why workshop design is such an important art to master. Of course, the best workshop facilitators know when to let go of the initial design and can iterate a workshop on the fly when things go off the rails. I have learned the hard way as a facilitator to ask for legitimacy to act at the beginning of a workshop: to interrupt, stick to time, or change activities to achieve results. Armed with that agreement, you have true permission to facilitate.

Great workshops are very different from the meetings we – unfortunately – still see in many organizations today. That's why Alison's book is so timely. Great workshops create deep engagement and get people involved. They use strong artifacts to create a shared understanding. They are designed to create tangible results. Once you put them at the centre of the way you work, they become your organizational culture.

Enjoy Alison's book to make workshops part of your company culture.

Alex Osterwalder, Lonay, Switzerland, August 2023

Introduction

What would it be like if you knew you and your colleagues could go to work, thrive and perform at your best? What if work was a place you went to develop and be fulfilled, not only professionally but also personally? What if you left work energized and excited, knowing that throughout your day you'd had moments of nourishing collaboration as well as the space to think and be creative? If you were confident that your team was aligned, yet you were all able to contribute in your own individual way that harnessed everyone's unique expertise, and enabled each of you to make a valuable contribution. What if you felt each day was productive, focused, and that you had made progress?

You might not have experienced this every day of your working life, but there is a chance that you have experienced it temporarily – like when you left a really great, expertly facilitated, collaborative workshop. If this is the case, you might have had your first insight into the potential of 'workshop culture'.

As a facilitator, I've sometimes wished I could bottle up the energy from the end of a great workshop and release it into the rest of an organization, so that a team can continue to feel it long after the sticky notes and flip-chart paper have been cleared away. This book is my attempt to help you make that happen. There's something about the energy, positivity, motivation and sense of momentum achieved in a workshop that can feel like a magic sauce. The way that the team has worked together, explored challenges, asked questions and found ways to express their creativity, opens up possibilities and hopes for the way forward.

Through my work, I've become well aware that this 'end-of-workshop' feeling is extremely difficult to maintain when teams get back to the realities of their daily work and to-do lists. Those periods of intense collaboration and focused discussion can resolve problems in a way that doesn't seem possible when everyone is back to business-as-usual.

Our workplaces have evolved into environments where teamwork is a core part of the way work gets done. It's no longer optional, and we must find ways to maintain those collaborative conditions found in workshops in our day-to-day working lives. Teamwork has always been necessary, but now, the need for it has never been greater.

Not only is teamwork becoming a key component of the workplace, but it's also getting faster, more complex and more intense than in the past. The world of work in a more industrialized era used to be pretty straightforward. The complexity was in product development, and once that was cracked, the execution was predictable and repeatable. In our current knowledge economy, the core of our work is solving problems and generating new ideas. Technology has increased the pace of change dramatically, and a growing need for innovation also brings a greater need for collaboration. Future-fit organizations cannot simply respond to changes, they must anticipate them. It's not just a matter of keeping up but of staying ahead, and to do that, we need to bring diverse expertise together to address the challenges we're facing. This requires us to work differently. Smart organizations know that if they want to move fast and innovate, they need to find the best talent and then pay attention to the dynamics within their companies so that they can mobilize that talent to work together.

Getting teamwork right is now essential for business survival. As teams become more central to the success of our companies, we need to be well-versed in collaboration as a capability to get ahead. This includes building our understanding of great teamwork, developing new communication skills, handling the conflict that will inevitably come from bringing different disciplines together, knowing how to build trust quickly in small teams, how to kick off projects effectively and how to keep motivation high.

Despite the thousands of books and articles written on collaboration and teamwork, we still can't seem to get enough advice on how to work well together. Even with the vast number of digital tools that promise to make collaboration easier, it's still a topic that perplexes us. Teams continue to be troubled with miscommunication and misinterpretation. Personality clashes and politics get in the way of doing our best work, all while we're struggling with growing workloads, tighter deadlines and reduced resources. The ability to keep a healthy momentum going from the exciting idea-generation phase through to final completion seems like an insurmountable challenge.

There is a huge need for collaborative working, yet we're quite a way from doing it to the required level. In a *Harvard Business Review* article, Behnam Tabrizi shares that '75% of cross-functional teams are dysfunctional'.[1] The gap between our ability to collaborate seamlessly and our pressing need for seamless collaboration is growing ever wider. It's time to look at teamwork differently and take it more seriously than ever before. The challenge is that there is no easy step-by-step guide, no silver bullet and no shortcuts. If we want to get better at collaboration, we need to put in the work.

My aim is that this book will show you where to focus your energy, make the process a little easier, and help you to build the mindset and skills needed to set up enduring success in your teams. It gives you a framework that works for now, and I also hope it will mark the beginning of a lifelong practice that evolves as you need it to. It will change the way you think about and approach your work. You will build a muscle memory for how to facilitate great collaboration that will stay with you throughout the rest of your career.

My experience

This book comes from my experience (and love of) facilitating workshops with teams as a way to help them work better together. I've always been a big advocate for collaboration, which is how my company, Bracket, was born. I could see what would happen when we got the right people together for the right task and created the right conditions for them to do what they do best.

I found my way to workshops not because I wanted to run them, but because it seemed the most logical way of kicking off a team project. A good workshop enabled me to work with teams to both gather the content and ideas for *what* they would do together, and set the expectations for *how* they would collaborate successfully to get the job done. Bringing teams together at the start, and building a project together from the ground up, seemed to empower people and create a good foundation for collaboration from then onwards. That's when I fell in love with the workshop format. I gained a lot of energy from motivating people in this way – guiding them to work out their own processes, which would lead them to be more invested in what they were working on. And it seemed to give them energy too.

The more I did this, the more I noticed the impact it had, especially with teams that were new to workshops. I could see how they transformed to become more collaborative, creative and communicative. They shifted the way they worked to break through blocks and barriers together. They built a deeper trust in one another and felt empowered to contribute ideas, and there was a clear positive impact on individuals when their ideas were valued.

When I wrote my first book, *Effective Workshops*, my main aim was to help more people run workshops with their teams. Workshops were a practical format, with clear outcomes during which you could get a lot done in a short space of time. Yet, I was aware that these were one-off engagements. I started to ask myself: if this was such a transformative experience for teams, and if we needed collaboration so badly, why were facilitated workshops the only chance teams were getting to experience this way of working?

When I had the opportunity to facilitate multiple workshops with a team, I could see the benefit this had on what they were working towards. I could also see that when teams were experiencing this consistently, it improved the way they worked together overall. The types of interactions they had in the workshop expanded beyond the session. They communicated more openly, they experimented, they asked questions, they involved each other and work got done more effectively.

There was also something interesting to me about my role as the workshop facilitator. My aim was to encourage people to be their most creative and productive selves. To me, it reflected the type of leadership that modern organizations need – nudging and supporting people in teams to work better together, designing an environment that enables great work, asking the questions that draw the best out of people, and ensuring everyone is heard.

This curiosity led me to explore how workshops can be a starting point for a high-performing collaborative team and the knock-on effect this could have. A great workshop is essentially an intense version of great teamwork. People come together for a marked period of time with a specific aim, to reach a specific outcome. There is a balance between generating ideas and, with the support of a facilitator, synthesizing them into something tangible. I've spent the last few years unpicking the elements of a successful workshop and using the same principles to help the teams I work with beyond a one-time event. I call this 'workshop culture'.

What is a 'workshop culture'?

Workshop culture = a team culture that uses the principles and practices of workshops and facilitation to encourage creativity and productivity, and to build the environment for effective collaboration.

I'm introducing the definition of a workshop culture early on, because most of this book will be highly practical and cover how to implement one. In my experience of working with teams, it's not the concept of collaboration that they struggle with, it's making it happen in practice.

Teams that have a workshop culture pay attention to how they meet and communicate, and intentionally design how they work together. A workshop culture is unique for each team. It puts people at the centre of the process and creates an environment for everyone to be equally heard and do their best work. All expertise is valued. Each individual knows why they are there and how their contribution matters.

The team also has open and transparent communication. Work alternates between collaborative discussions and individual focused work. Everyone knows what they are collectively working towards and where they need to go for information. Meetings are meaningful and interactive, and each session has a clear purpose. There is a bias towards forward momentum and understanding how every interaction will help the team get to the next stage.

A workshop culture is respectful, but doesn't avoid healthy conflict for the sake of consensus. The team is not afraid to address tricky problems together. It's not seamless – there will be moments that feel uncertain, but a workshop culture means being comfortable with ambiguity, and being guided through it by using facilitation. It is about getting everyone involved and making progress.

The presence of the word 'workshop' does not mean that this only applies to teams that are physically co-located. As you'll see, the responsive nature of a workshop culture is relevant whether a team is in an office together, fully remote or a hybrid of the two.

Collaboration is a broad concept, but it becomes more concrete when we match it to what happens in a great workshop. Workshop culture is based on the principle that workshops can be more than a one-off event – they are a vehicle to a high-performing team. When run well and consistently, workshops lead teams to be happier and more engaged, and eventually transform the way they work together overall.

How to use this book

You might be a team leader wanting to instil a healthier culture in your team, a team member wanting to do the same, a CEO or a HR professional. Whatever your reason for picking up this book, I want to give you the tools to transform how you work. The great thing about building a workshop culture is that anyone, at any level in an organization, can initiate it, and you don't need to be a seasoned facilitator. You can start with a few simple tools, and I will share them throughout this book.

However, this is about much more than how to run great workshops. We'll explore how starting with this seemingly small intervention creates a ripple effect throughout a team, and how this leads a company to become a better place to work. Many of us are just trying to make small improvements to our everyday working lives. This book will show you how to achieve this.

Part 1 identifies the problem that workshop culture solves. Chapter 1 digs into the true challenge of collaboration and its impact. Chapter 2 explores why workshops form the basis of great team cultures, deconstructs workshops and outlines the factors that we need to recreate in our teams.

Part 2 introduces you to the principles behind a workshop culture. Chapter 3 considers what it feels and looks like and the core foundations, and Chapter 4 looks at the skills and mindsets of the people, individuals like you, who want to lead and drive this change. This chapter prepares you to introduce a workshop culture to your team.

Part 3 provides a practical five-pillar framework for building a workshop culture and a high-performing team. It looks at how teams can build the ability and discipline to have better conversations and create new ways of working together. Chapters 5 to 9 each cover a pillar of the framework. The five pillars are as follows:

1. **Alignment:** how to align your team around a vision and core values (Chapter 5).
2. **Cohesion:** connecting your team through empathy and a deep appreciation for the diversity each person brings (Chapter 6).
3. **Communication:** the role of effective meetings in building a workshop culture (Chapter 7).
4. **Design:** how to build new ways of working (Chapter 8).
5. **Change:** embedding a workshop culture through sustainable behaviour change (Chapter 9).

Throughout these five chapters, you'll see how it's completely possible to create a workshop culture in your team even if it's not fully present across the wider organization. It will impact your and your immediate colleagues' experience of working life.

Although you may feel the team level is as far as your influence goes, when you start to implement a workshop culture, you may find that the results attract attention. Colleagues from outside your team will be interested to learn more. Finally, in the conclusion, we'll explore what a workshop culture could look like when embedded across an organization and the opportunities it brings.

Throughout the book you'll read anonymized case studies from real life, forward-thinking leaders and teams that have introduced elements of a workshop culture. I hope that these case studies, together with the highly practical tips throughout the book, will help you to make impactful change.

REFLECTION: before we start

You are reading this book because you are curious about creating better ways of working for your team. Let's start with your future vision.

- How do you want your team to work together?
- What is happening daily, weekly, monthly and yearly?
- How does it feel?
- What experience do you want to create for your team?

PART 1

IDENTIFYING THE PROBLEM

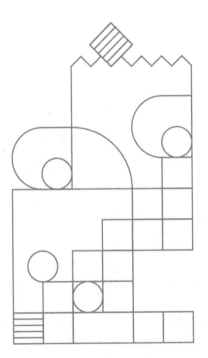

In Part 1, we take a deep dive into the problems our modern organizations are facing and connect these challenges to the potential solution of workshops.

Chapter 1

The impact of the problem

In Chapter 1, we'll address the challenge of collaboration and what happens when we don't get it right. We'll see how ineffective meetings are not just wasted time, they have a real impact on our working experience. We'll look at what truly engages people at work and why every organization needs to consider purpose and meaning as part of their culture.

By the end of this chapter you will have learnt:

- what is stopping us from truly collaborating effectively
- the impact of badly-run meetings, and why it's essential to address them
- the relationship between performance and engagement at work.

The challenge of true collaboration

Modern organizations in the knowledge economy need people to work together effectively. A 2019 Deloitte study showed that 53% of respondents found that shifting towards a team-based organizational model from more hierarchical structures results in a significant improvement in performance.[1]

We fully grasp collaboration as a concept – what it means and what it looks like. We instinctively know the differences between good and bad collaboration. We understand that open communication, sharing and transparency form the basis of healthy teamwork. So why do so many teams still struggle to make it happen? It's because the effort required for successful collaboration is often misunderstood. It is not something that just happens on its own – it can be tremendously hard to implement in practice. True collaboration requires change at the individual, team and organizational level.

At the individual level, it can feel easier and quicker to do things alone rather than inviting the views of someone else that might take your work in a different, but potentially better, direction. (As the saying goes, 'If you want to go fast, go alone. If you want to go far, go together').

In teams, different personalities, ways of working and perspectives introduce complexity, and when this isn't handled well, troubled dynamics occur. The motivation to weather these challenges wanes without a clear, collective goal. When we have a longer-term view with our team, we can stick with collaboration through bumps and barriers. Without this, it's more challenging, especially against the backdrop of urgent demands on our time.

At the organizational level, often structures and processes do not encourage collaboration. For example, when individuals are mainly rewarded through an upwards career path, organizations unintentionally make collaboration a lower priority, and may even foster competition. Collaboration might be the more rational approach for leveraging knowledge and expertise, but it becomes harder to prioritize if it's not a formal part of compensation. Ideally the most effective and fulfilling collaboration is driven internally – people on the team are determined to make it work because it makes sense to do so. But collaborative working is more likely to be valued when an organization's systems are set up to recognize it.

If collaboration is such a big part of our working experience, what is the real impact of getting it wrong? We'll explore three ways that substandard collaboration can hurt a company – bad meetings, low engagement and lack of purpose.

Impact 1: bad meetings

Bad meetings waste time and money

Any company that relies on interactions between people to get things done needs moments when those people come together to discuss their work. But meetings are often viewed as a necessary evil. They take up a lot of the working day, and are often seen as a distraction from the work that people really need and want to do. In the US, employees average about six hours per week in meetings (for senior managers this can be up to 23 hours).[2] In 2019 the meeting-scheduling software company Doodle estimated that poorly organized meetings would cost more than $450 billion across the UK and US.[3] Any organization wanting to make a widespread change that impacts everyone should look at their meetings.

However, the problem is not the meetings themselves, it's how they are run. We need meetings to collaborate, so how can we make them feel like a key part of work where important discussions take place?

Meetings impact performance

Bad meetings impact performance on an individual and team level. An employee may feel that they can't perform at their best because of the endless interruptions from meetings. But various studies have also shown that the effectiveness of a meeting is linked to team performance and organizational success.

In their research, Kauffeld and Lehmann-Willenbrock used analysis software together with questionnaires and interviews to determine the success of meetings they were monitoring. They found that a positive meeting, which they defined as including constructive interactions such as 'problem-solving and action planning', can have an impact on the team's performance and success up to two and a half years following the meeting! When teams experienced more dysfunctional interactions, such as criticizing others or complaining, the negative effects on the organization were greater.[4]

This pattern – the negative-to-positive interaction ratio – exists elsewhere. For example, Gottman and Levensen's research on relationships found that successful partnerships need a ratio of five positive interactions to every negative one to reset the balance.[5] If we are seeing a similar phenomenon in our meetings, then it's clear that we must work harder to enhance our meeting experience so that they do not harm our team and organizational performance.

Meetings impact how we feel about our work

Meetings have a direct impact on how we feel about our work, which in turn affects our engagement. As discovered by Mroz et al. in 2018, 'meeting satisfaction has been noted to be a significant, distinct predictor of employee job satisfaction'.[6] Who would have thought that we have the power to create a better working life just through addressing the way that we meet?

Imagine the difference between a meeting that gives you energy and a meeting that depletes your energy. You can leave a meeting feeling that it's been a good use of time, buzzing with ideas, with new knowledge, and motivated to take action. At meetings like this, you feel like a valued member of the group. In contrast, a meeting that depletes your energy leaves you feeling that you could have spent your time in another way, that your workload has been unnecessarily added to, or you may even feel that you weren't needed there at all.

Workshop facilitators are well aware of what happens to someone's esteem when they've had the chance to share their ideas and know they have been listened to. There is something valuable about knowing that your contribution was appreciated. It's a form of recognition and validation, and contributes to our sense of belonging at work. Since 93% of employees who feel valued are motivated to do their best work,[7] even just shifting this balance in our meetings can make a difference.

Rogelberg et al. (2010) also found a connection between an employee's satisfaction with their meetings and how satisfied they feel about their job. They highlighted the role of managers and the importance of providing training for them to develop the right skills to lead meetings effectively.[8] A few years later, Allen et al. (2013) concluded that managers can make some very simple fixes to address bad meetings – starting and ending meetings on time, ensuring open communication and ensuring meetings are relevant.[9] Think of how this could affect employee retention or turnover. Companies could save valuable money, time and other resources that they lose when a staff member leaves, by putting the right effort into running better meetings.

Change your meetings, change your culture

Given the clear link between meetings, company performance and employee engagement, it's surprising that more organizations do not take a formal approach to improve them. Whether intentionally or not, meetings form the backbone of an organization. They can give you a snapshot of a company or team's culture. Whatever happens in meetings is most likely a reflection of what's happening in the wider culture. So, if you can take the pulse of an organization by observing its meetings, can what happens in a meeting also impact the team and company culture? Yes. And this presents us with a great opportunity.

Most companies are not aware of the potential for change, and so take a passive approach – meetings just happen, and are not actively designed. But for a practice that forms so much of the working day, we can transform our companies if we make them a fully functional part of the culture. Some leading technology companies such as Dropbox, Asana, Shopify and Zapier have even experimented with a 'meeting reset' – wiping all internal meetings from their calendars.[10] We don't all need to be as radical as this. It's about optimizing the way our existing meetings are run to make the most of the time people spend together.

Meetings are an opportunity to set the tone and environment for collaboration. They are a time to tap into collective knowledge where people can feel heard, can reconnect and can engage with their work. They don't have to be a time for aimless discussion – they can be a means for getting real work done. When designed well, they might even be something that people look forward to – where they can express their creative ideas and get the support they need from their colleagues, contributing to a positive experience of work.

If meetings *are* a reflection of a team's culture, workshops are a snapshot of what it *could* look like. By being aware and making some small shifts, changes to the way we meet will kickstart the momentum to improve our team's culture.

Impact 2: low engagement

The extent of low engagement

In 2017, Gallup published a report that sent a shockwave through the world of work. They found that 85% of employees were not engaged or were actively disengaged at work.[11] Only 15% of workers at the time were enjoying their work and fulfilling their potential.

This statistic was alarming in itself but even more so because the connection between employee engagement and a healthy business bottom line was already known. A 2002 research paper showed a clear relationship between employee engagement and business outcomes, demonstrating that business units with higher employee engagement had a 70% higher performance success rate than those that showed below median employee engagement.[12] Companies that hadn't been doing enough to engage and support their employees were missing out on potential success as a result.

The idea that employees are solely responsible for their own happiness and engagement at work is no longer fit for our companies. Savvy leaders know that if they want sustained, long-term high performance and the results that come with it, they need to ensure they create great places to work. And this doesn't need to cost the earth. There is no one that this is more obvious to than Michael C. Bush, CEO of Great Place to Work, an organization committed to recognizing and rewarding those companies that put their people first. In a short TED video he explains how 'Organizations that have a lot of happy employees have three times the revenue growth, compared to organizations where that's not true.'[13] And the things that make it happen? Trust and respect, fairness, and listening. Things that cost nothing at all.[14]

The fact that many high-performance work environments are characterized by toxicity, stress and burnout may lead us to believe that when we have a happy environment, performance is a lower priority. Is it possible to have a high-performing team that is also happy and engaged and puts people first?

A happy, engaged culture and high performance are not mutually exclusive. In fact they can support each other, but they need careful balance and attention. As the 2002 research paper mentioned above showed, there is a clear link between productivity and engagement in the workplace, but it's sometimes hard to ascertain which needs to come first.

While we do need to put people first, which in turn contributes to the performance of the company, that doesn't mean that we do it at the expense of the company's stability and success. A company needs to perform well to provide jobs. The culture created needs to support the business's goals to keep it going, growing and making a positive impact.

We don't just want to create *nice* places to work. We want to create *better* places to work which support the financial performance of our businesses. And the way to do that sustainably is to look after and value the people within it.

High engagement does lead to higher performance, and when the environment exists for people to be their most creative and productive, that leads to happiness and engagement. When people can just get on with the work they love, we're more likely to build a much happier team, and this creates an upward spiral for more creativity and productivity as shown in Figure 1.1.

Figure 1.1 The cyclical nature of engagement and performance.

This mirrors the findings of Teresa Amabile and Steven Kramer, which they write about in their book, *The Progress Principle: Using Small Wins to Ignite Joy, Engagement, and Creativity at Work*. After reviewing 11,000 daily diary entries of 438 knowledge workers, they found that the most important factor in creating a happy and engaged workplace was enabling progress and removing barriers and blockers.[15] Workers, particularly in the knowledge sector, want to be able to do their work and to do it well.

In team cultures, we overestimate the value of perks such as free lunches, cool furniture and branded swag, and underestimate the value of providing the environment for people to get on with their best work without unnecessary obstacles. This is what impacts their satisfaction.

Impact 3: lack of purpose

The drive towards purposeful careers

People want more purposeful careers. In 2018, the coaching platform BetterUp reported that nine out of ten people would reduce their pay in return for more meaningful work.[16] For the amount of time the average employee spends at work (about one-third of their lives), it makes sense that they would want to spend it feeling fulfilled. We want more from our workplaces. We do not want to be seen merely as a 'human resource'. We want to *feel* good and know that we have *done* good. We don't just want to clock up hours in a soulless cycle of task delivery.

This realization has led people to make drastic changes. In 2021, publications started to report on the 'Great Resignation'. It seemed that the Covid-19 pandemic had prompted millions of people to re-evaluate how they spent their time. In the US alone, over 47 million people resigned from their jobs in 2021.[17] But it wasn't just the pandemic. This 'corporate exodus' had been bubbling away under the surface for a long time – there had already been predictions that the freelancer market would rise to 50% of the workforce in the US by 2027.[18] It was almost becoming a rite of passage: you would work your way up in a corporate career and reach a turning point where you leave to set up your own company for more flexibility, freedom and autonomy. At the time of writing this book, in 2023, it seems that now, more than ever, employers need to take purpose and meaning more seriously so that they can attract and retain talent.

Purpose is essential for personal well-being

Having purpose and meaning at work is not just a nice-to-have, fuzzy exercise. It has a real impact on our individual well-being. Let's not underestimate this. In 2022, *The Economist* reported that 59% of workers would 'consider taking a job that offers better well-being benefits than their current employer'.[19] A 2020 study on individual purpose by McKinsey showed that employees who feel that their work fulfils their purpose have better outcomes in work and in life.[20] This in turn contributes to our team health, which leads to overall organizational success.

As the crossover between work and personal life becomes more blurred, we do need to become more disciplined about keeping boundaries for our own well-being and happiness. At the same time, we want workplaces where we can fulfil our potential. When we are fulfilled at work, this has an impact on how we feel about our lives; and when we feel good about our lives, that has further reaching impact in our families, communities and society at large. We need to think more about the significance of creating work environments where people can grow, learn, develop and provide an opportunity for them to make a difference.

Why are you implementing a workshop culture?

We'll now return to the topic of creating a workshop culture. We've explored why collaboration is necessary, how it's hard to implement in practice and the impact of ineffective collaboration on an organization. A workshop culture starts to address the root cause of the challenge of true collaboration.

When we're thinking about why we want to introduce a workshop culture, we also need to consider the return on investment we will get for our efforts. Think deeply about your motivations for wanting to transform your team. Which of these three scenarios do you most identify with?

1. Your team is performing well and you want to do everything you can to keep it going. Creating a workshop culture would be like taking a vitamin – something that you do as a preventative measure to maintain your team's health.
2. There are some challenges in your team that you need to resolve, and you need some remedies. Workshop culture would be your painkiller. Your desire for a workshop culture is strong because you need to see a change.
3. You are somewhere in between these two ends of the scale.

Regardless of the angle you're approaching this from, as we saw in Figure 1.1, it's cyclical. If you want to create a workshop culture for more creativity and productivity, in the process you'll create a happier and more engaged working environment. If you're doing it primarily because you want more happiness and engagement in your team, then the knock-on effect will be increased creativity and productivity.

TRY THIS: evaluate your meetings

As this chapter has shown, meetings are a good place to start if you want to shift towards a workshop culture, and we'll explore this more in Chapter 7. They are one of the most prominent touchpoints for a team, and we can take techniques directly from workshops to influence the way we interact in these sessions.

To kickstart the process, observe your meetings and reflect on the following questions:

- What are the dynamics between people in the meeting? How do people respond to each other? Are there a few people dominating the conversation?

- How comfortable are people with each other? Do they feel safe speaking up? Is anyone reluctant to contribute?

- Is everyone contributing their ideas, and is creativity encouraged? Do people support and build on each other's ideas or immediately criticize them?

- If in a physical space, how are people positioned around the room? Does the layout give preference and attention to a select few?

- Are people engaged in what's going on? Are they listening to each other intently, or are they distracted? Are they working hard to get noticed, or are they taking a back seat and trying to make themselves invisible?

- Is the meeting itself productive? How are people progressing through the conversation? Are there clear actions, or is discussion going around in never-ending cycles?

- What is the mood at the end of the meeting? Do people seem energized or drained? Motivated or disheartened?

- Overall, what is your team's approach to running meetings? How often do you meet? What types of meetings do you have? How much time do you spend in meetings?

Chapter 1 – key takeaways:

- Collaboration is not a difficult concept to understand, but we struggle to implement it in practice.
- We can change our experience of work if we address ineffective collaboration.
- Bad meetings impact performance and engagement, and if we improve our meetings, we can improve our culture.
- A happy and engaged culture is not mutually exclusive from a high-performing one.

So many organizations cite the importance of collaboration, and so it deserves proper attention. This is where we can learn greatly from workshops, which is the topic of the next chapter.

Chapter 2

Why workshops are the solution

In this chapter, we'll outline some of the ingredients of great workshops to demonstrate how they are a real solution to the challenges we've just explored in Chapter 1. We'll look at how workshops support teamwork through elements such as encouraging equal contributions and engagement, open communication, visible progress and curiosity, learning and experimentation. Then we'll consider the team environment we want to create, and unpack the specific factors we'll be designing to achieve a workshop culture.

By the end of this chapter, you will have learnt:

- how great workshops support collaboration and better team relationships
- the characteristics of high-performing teams.

CASE STUDY: how I discovered workshop culture

I haven't always been aware of the power of workshops to transform team culture. It's something that gradually emerged in my practice as a workshop facilitator. Clients would hire me to support a discussion they were having, and once the workshop finished, so did my role. My entire service consisted of impactful, one-off engagements.

Then came a new opportunity. A client wanted to formalize their brand identity to support recruitment, and they asked me to help them create their company values. We started off with a small group of executives, including the CEO, and discussed their early ideas.

This workshop was completely content-focused. We wanted to generate a list of values to take forward, and that's exactly what we did. The team shared stories that typified the company, we captured words and phrases using sticky notes, identified themes and voted.

The client – a professional services firm – asked me to come back to do the same exercise with a wider group of senior executives during their monthly strategy meeting. They wanted to see if what had emerged in the small group workshop reflected the views of the whole team. I packed up my workshop materials and travelled to their head office. I had been allocated a two-hour slot in their full-day meeting after lunch, and I waited outside the room until they were ready for me.

When I walked into the room, I was faced with the longest conference table I'd ever seen, with 20-plus people seated around it. This was their usual way of running their strategy meeting – a bit of business, a bit of lunch and some social connection – and it worked for them. But for an external facilitator like me, who needed their attention for a focused discussion, it could be a challenge.

The CEO sat at one end of the table and chaired the meeting. He owned the agenda, and the majority of information came from him. They shared how they hardly ever got through the full agenda, which was usually a mix of strategic issues and daily challenges. They frequently got caught up in discussion loops and never really heard from everyone around the table. Not surprising, as the length of the table was intimidating!

What I was about to do would shake up their idea of how a meeting should and could be run. I dropped sticky notes and coloured marker pens around the table. I stood at one end of the room with the flip chart. I led this larger group through the same exercises

I had done in the previous meeting, and asked them to split into smaller groups of three or four to share their thoughts. We worked quickly, there was animated discussion and laughter, and everyone chipped in.

By the end of the session, we had created values similar to the original group, demonstrating a strong company identity. But that wasn't the biggest takeaway. This was the first time that the senior team had experienced such a meeting together, and I was surprised that it had so much impact. Before this workshop, I hadn't realized my power as a facilitator to break down existing traditions and constructs.

I was invited back to another strategy meeting to help the senior team connect the values to the vision of the company, and then invited again to help identify ways to embed them throughout the company. Each time I was with this team, I saw how the members opened up a little more, got used to using sticky notes, coloured markers and breakout discussions. It felt like a transformation was happening, slowly.

And that wasn't the end. I'd hear how connections had sparked after the workshops as a result of the conversations we had. The senior team audited their meetings and introduced new formats where they would discuss daily challenges more frequently. This meant that they could spend the strategy meeting discussing higher-level issues. They even introduced a Friday meeting for 'ideas and innovation'. The workshops I'd run had started a snowball effect of connection, thinking and progress.

And that's when it clicked for me – a workshop is not just about what happens in the room. There is so much more potential, if we allow it.

Why great workshops lead to great team cultures

Now we'll break down the characteristics of a workshop so that we can see how it is relevant to a team culture. These characteristics are:

- true collaboration
- facilitation
- equal contributions and engagement
- open communication and visible progress
- curiosity, learning and experimentation
- responsiveness, emergence and iteration
- tolerance of ambiguity and uncertainty.

True collaboration

The fundamental drive behind workshops is to encourage collaboration, and as we have seen, this is what modern organizations need. Workshops give us the opportunity to experience what true collaboration is. If we see collaboration as a skill, workshops are a place where we can practice. The more we do it, the more we improve. With a good structure and great facilitation, teams are able to quickly start working together towards a common goal. It's not necessarily a smooth process, but it creates an environment that allows different minds to come together and solve complex problems.

True collaboration is where everyone can contribute individually and equally with their brilliant talents and perspectives. Yet in the final outcome, it may be hard to distinguish those individual contributions – everyone's thoughts and ideas have combined to create something new and better. What's more, in true collaboration, the contributors aren't concerned with being recognized for their specific ideas, because they know it has been a true collaborative effort to get there. Yet, each person is still celebrated for their participation.

Facilitation

The paradox of workshops is that when a facilitator does a great job, it actually looks like they aren't doing very much at all! Participants will be so focused on what they are creating together that they may not realize how much the facilitator is doing in the background to monitor the group dynamics and make sure discussions stay on point. Although their presence might be subtle on the day, the facilitator has likely worked extremely hard beforehand to design a session that is right for the group.

A workshop facilitator is not the same as someone who chairs a meeting. A meeting chair usually owns the agenda and will control the conversation. This role often falls to the most senior person in the room. By contrast, a facilitator plays an objective role, guides the conversation, and ensures full involvement from everyone. They do this by asking questions and encouraging participation without getting involved in the discussion themselves. A facilitator does not need to be a content expert, because it's not their job to do the actual work. Instead they create the space for the workshop attendees to problem-solve together. This leads the participants to feel more autonomy and engagement.

Imagine what might happen when a leader adopts this approach for their team – taking a step back from creating the work outputs and instead empowering their team to step up and take the stage together. This is covered in more detail in Chapter 4.

Equal contributions and engagement

A workshop levels the playing field in terms of the seniority of team members, gender identity, ethnicity and any other factors that bring diversity to a team. As well as ensuring a fair representation in the room, a facilitated workshop strives for inclusion, ensuring that everyone has

the opportunity to have their voice heard. Workshops are 'flat' environments where all ideas are equally respected regardless of who they
came from. Team members will engage more if they feel their expertise
is valued and they are fully able to use their talent and expertise.

This has a profound impact on team culture. First, a facilitated
approach can work to dismantle any unhelpful hierarchy or power
dynamics in the room, particularly the problem of HiPPOs (highly
paid person's opinions). It's not true that only the most senior people
in an organization have the best ideas.

Second, promoting the concept that ideas can come from
anywhere enables a team to maximize its real potential. A 2018 study
from Gallup shows that only 29% of workers feel that they're expected
to be creative at work.[1] It's common to find untapped ideas and
underutilized knowledge in a workforce that simply need the space
to be unleashed. Providing people with the opportunity to share their
views is the first step to innovation. Employees feel fulfilled, and the
business benefits as a result.

Open communication and visible progress

Often when people think of workshops, particularly idea-generation
workshops, they associate them with lots of sticky notes, whiteboards
and flipcharts (and more recently, their digital counterparts – online
whiteboards). While an abundance of coloured-paper squares isn't
always a sign of a successful session, there's a reason why workshops
are associated with these tools. There is something very powerful about
recording ideas and bringing them to life – moving them from simple
concepts in our head to something more real. This can be in text form
or visual, but capturing the discussion in these ways has many advantages. In *Gamestorming: A Playbook for Innovators, Rulebreakers and
Changemakers*, Gray, Brown and Macanufo refer to these as 'artifacts'.
They explain the benefits of having information in a physical form
rather than holding it in our memory: 'artifacts make information

explicit, tangible, portable and persistent'.[2] 'Artifacts' help discussions to be more productive. When people talk around objects and visualizations, this helps ideas and concepts to land more easily.

Aside from the basic need of recording the discussion for a team to refer back to, it also demonstrates to participants that their ideas have been noted. It visualizes progress, and the team can clearly see how much and what they have covered. The team can use the content to make connections between different ideas and highlight any tension points to address. It can help to reduce duplication and provide a sense of collective ownership in the workshop outcomes.

It's not only workshops that use this format. Think of war rooms – physical team spaces filled with sketches, notes and visuals dedicated to keeping teams up to date with any project developments (although I'd debate the use of the term 'war room' – no one is actually going to battle!). Now we have a number of tools, such as Mural, Miro and Google Jamboard, that enable us to do this digitally. Unsurprisingly, the wider collaborative whiteboard software market is predicted to see further growth, expecting to increase from $2,160.66 million in 2023 to an estimated $4,901.31 million in 2028 as we see a move towards more remote and hybrid ways of working.[3]

Making work visible in this way keeps communication open and transparent. The whole team can always stay involved and aware of what is happening. Anyone can highlight potential problems, and work becomes more fluid and connected, and can happen more quickly.

Curiosity, learning and experimentation

An effective workshop sets the tone for people to explore and challenge the status quo. We feel safe to share ideas early and in their ugly, unfinished state. It's like a sandpit where we can play, experiment, make and break things. We have permission to make mistakes, and there is no pressure to say the 'right' thing. Participants know that they are learning together, and they will leave with new insights – a reframing of a problem they were grappling with or even a new piece of knowledge they can use in their work.

Curiosity is essential for modern business. A 2018 study reported in *Harvard Business Review* stated: 'In the survey of more than 3,000 employees … 92% credited curious people with bringing new ideas into teams and organizations and viewed curiosity as a catalyst for job satisfaction, motivation, innovation, and high performance.'[4] Workshops are a great opportunity to cultivate learning and curiosity. The more people are exposed to curiosity, the more they can understand how to apply it in their daily work.

There are many creativity techniques that facilitators use in their workshops to help teams think differently. Workshops encourage us to use questions to challenge ourselves and explore together. An example of this is the 'how might we …?' exercise used in design thinking (which I will refer to more in Chapters 4 and 8). Design thinking is an experimental and empathetic approach to product and service development, and is defined by the consultancy IDEO as 'a human-centred approach to innovation'.[5] When 'how might we …?' is used at the beginning of a question, it encourages a team to consider possibilities ('how'), without the immediate need for a final solution ('might'), and collectively ('we') when problem-solving. For example: *how might we* improve our meetings? Or, *how might we* share information more effectively? When people are introduced to this structure in a workshop and can see its impact, it becomes a tool for them to use in their regular conversations.

Responsiveness, emergence and iteration

Despite the hard work that goes into creating a workshop outline, a facilitator will still hold it lightly during a session. A team may need to spend more time than planned on one topic, or they may need to change direction completely. Something significant could come up during a discussion that the group must pay attention to before moving on. The nature of a workshop is that everyone can shift and regroup as necessary.

While there must be a structure and process to support and bring people together, there must also be a recognition and willingness to change it when it is no longer relevant. A facilitator supports the group in becoming more comfortable with this need in order to adapt to what emerges.

A workshop provides the practice ground for teams to become more responsive in a low-risk environment. Then they build more resilience and develop the ability to deal with unexpected disruption. For example, a team might develop and align on their strategy and what they will focus on for the year ahead, but outside influences may force them to rethink this six months on (as the phrase goes, 'no plan survives contact with the real world'). This ability to respond to situations and stay grounded in the face of change is a key requirement for teams and companies of the future.

Tolerance of ambiguity and uncertainty

There's something about a workshop that gives people permission to be messy. Whereas in their usual work people may strive for perfection, in a workshop they don't mind scribbling things down, crossing them out, sketching out rough concepts, or being surrounded by unfinished ideas and thoughts.

What would happen if we took this same creative mindset back to the everyday? This mess doesn't have to manifest physically, but we can still understand that creativity is a non-linear process that requires exploration, discovery, getting things wrong, throwing ideas away, screwing them up and starting again. Our companies need new ideas, but creativity can feel chaotic. We need to be able to tolerate the uncomfortable feeling that comes with not knowing the answer right away or not forming perfectly shaped ideas from the outset.

Workshops may look unorganized to an outside observer, but they often have a carefully crafted structure. As a result, it is more likely – more than in a traditionally run meeting – to get to the desired outcomes of creativity, productivity and innovation. Workshops can be high energy, and granted, it's not possible to work at this intensity for long periods of time. But we can take a lot from how we design and lead workshops, and apply it to how we design and lead our teams for better results all round. This is what a workshop culture achieves.

What you are designing for in a workshop culture

To start considering how your team will work together as a result of a workshop culture you first need to get clear on the environment you are designing. What makes a great team culture? These are the same elements that make workshops great.

Psychological safety

Psychological safety is the idea that every team member feels safe to speak up, make mistakes and take risks in front of their teammates. The concept became widely known as a result of a 2012 internal research study by Google – Project Aristotle – where they sought to identify the characteristics of high-performing teams.[6] But the term was originally conceptualized in 1999 by Amy Edmondson – a Harvard Business School academic.[7] The Google research identified that high-performing individuals have less of an impact on the success of a team than the presence of psychological safety. This demonstrated that *how* a team works together has more of an impact on the success of a team than *who* is on the team and *what* they are working on. It's clear to see how psychological safety can have positive implications for many aspects of teamwork, including getting better ideas, being more open, building trust and supporting diversity.

Workshop facilitators aim to create an environment where everyone feels able to contribute without any kind of negative impact. Sometimes this is the primary reason they are invited to work with a team. They spend a lot of time designing for psychological safety, as the success of a workshop almost depends on it. This is a key principle to carry over into a workshop culture.

When there is psychological safety, team members are more willing to experiment and step outside of their comfort zone, which could lead to significant benefits. For example, they may be more prepared to try out a risky idea that, if successful, could lead to a breakthrough or innovation for the team.

REFLECTION: does your team have psychological safety?

Questions to ask:

- What happens when someone makes a mistake on your team?
- What is your team's attitude to failure?
- How frequently do team members share early ideas, even if they are not quite thought through?
- How regularly do members of your team step outside of their comfort zone?
- How often does your team truly innovate?

Diversity

Diverse teams make better teams – for creativity and innovation, for making better decisions and for performance.[8] Our ability to solve complex challenges relies on bringing people together with different viewpoints that have formed from their professional and personal experiences. It makes our discussions more rich and interesting, and reaps better results. Ensuring diversity in a team is just the first step –

the views must then be surfaced. The outcomes are better, but it can be a challenging path, as there is more opportunity for conflict when people are exposed to new perspectives.

In a workshop culture, this means celebrating differences. It means appreciating that uncomfortable moments can create opportunity for a positive learning experience. It also requires the team to constantly examine and question inherent biases that might exist – for example applying more validity to ideas based on who they come from – and when biases surface, everyone must work to redress the balance.

REFLECTION: diverse thinking in your team

Questions to ask:

- How do we respond when we are challenged on our existing views?
- How can we create an environment that is safe for people to be themselves?
- What is our attitude towards those that disagree with the majority?

Healthy conflict

A workshop is a safe container for *productive* conflict. Without support and careful handling, we will naturally try to avoid conflict, but it can arise at any time when a new dynamic is introduced. Productive conflict around ideas and tasks is a defining feature for a high-performing collaborative environment and a workshop culture. To expect a team to exist without ever experiencing conflict is not only unrealistic but a real shame. We don't want everyone to think the same. We want people to challenge each other in a fruitful way.

Embracing conflict takes courage. How do we become more adventurous and see it as a challenge to work through rather than doing our best to avoid it? If we turn our backs on conflict, we risk missing out on some really great discussions and breakthroughs. A team must (1) acknowledge conflict as a normal and natural part of teamwork, even though it might initially feel uncomfortable, and (2) have tools and strategies for dealing with it, in the same way that a facilitator might in a workshop. For example, Edward de Bono's Six Thinking Hats is a wonderful tool for welcoming different perspectives in a systematic way.[9]

REFLECTION: do you know how to foster productive conflict?

Questions to ask:

- How do you deal with conflict when it arises?
- What methods do you have for encouraging productive conflict?
- Where and when can you discuss conflict as a natural part of teamwork?
- What do you do to ensure that healthy, productive and creative conflict is normalized within your team?

Autonomy

Part of the magic of workshops is the opportunity to show a team how they can work together, take initiative, and have more ownership over the outcomes. The facilitator clarifies the end goal and workshop purpose, and guides the process, but the team is responsible for what they create to get there. This creates a sense of confidence in the team for what they can do together. Knapp et al. explain how this is an additional outcome of the week-long sprint workshop framework that they developed while at Google Ventures. At the end of their book *Sprint: How to Solve Big Problems and Test New Ideas in Just Five Days* – a practical handbook to run the process – they state: 'After your first sprint, you might notice a shift in the way your team works ... You'll build confidence in one another's expertise and in your collective ability to make progress toward ambitious goals.'[10]

When people feel they have more autonomy over their work, they are more productive.[11] This idea may challenge those in more traditional and hierarchical organizations who are used to more command-and-control type management, but autonomy is not the same as complete chaos. In a workshop culture, it means giving people freedom over how they get their work done. Clear goal setting and personal accountability are still important – even more so. But people can make their choices about how they work based on what they know about themselves. Self-awareness and autonomy go hand in hand. When we're aware of our own productivity patterns, barriers, strengths and areas for improvement, we can design our own work to effectively get things done.

REFLECTION: creating more autonomy in your team

Questions to ask:

- How can you maintain and build accountability?
- How can you stay up to date with each other's work?
- How can you understand each other's working patterns so that you can work effectively together?
- How can you keep your team connected and aligned even though you might be working in your own different ways?

Transparency

In a team with high levels of autonomy, there is a greater need for transparency so that a team can stay aligned and up to date. As we've covered, one way this happens in workshops is to capture and display the content. There is power in being able to see what has been produced and discussed and being able to access it at any time. In a workshop culture, transparency is about making all work, statuses and information visible. This is not the same as micromanagement, and in fact has the opposite effect. Transparent teams are empowered teams. They can make their own decisions based on agreed criteria rather than having to pass everything through a manager or individual who holds all the information.

Transparency frees up time and supports productivity and progress, as it's easier for everyone on the team to find information. Encouraging people to share early and often reduces the chances of duplication and bottlenecks. With more transparency, a team can uncover potential conflict and problem-solve sooner so that it doesn't derail a project later on.

REFLECTION: introducing more transparency in your team

Questions to ask:

- How can we make necessary information visible to every team member?
- How can we make decision-making processes clear and record our decisions effectively?

Chapter 2 – key takeaways:

- Workshops are the solution to addressing ineffective collaboration in our organizations.
- How a team works together has more of an impact on its success than who is on the team and what they are working on.
- High-performing teams have psychological safety, diversity, healthy conflict and autonomy. Workshops show us how we can start to recreate those elements.

Hopefully, by now you are starting to get a sense of how learning from workshops can solve the problem of ineffective collaboration. We'll continue to unpack more of these elements throughout the rest of the book. Next, in Part 2, we'll dive into the mechanics of a workshop culture.

PART 2

INTRODUCING WORKSHOP CULTURE

Part 2 is all about exploring the workshop culture concept, illustrating what it looks and feels like, and preparing you to introduce it to your team.

Chapter 3

Understanding workshop culture

If you've ever visited a co-working space where you can feel the buzz of freelancers and entrepreneurs toiling away at their craft, then you have a sense of what a workshop culture looks like. It is entirely possible to build a workshop culture in a remote team, but if you were to observe this in a physical environment, the first thing you might notice is a palpable energy that you can see in everyone working there. This comes from the freedom and autonomy they experience in getting their work done and being trusted with their output.

However, a workshop culture is less about fancy offices and more about observing how team members interact with each other. In this chapter, we'll delve deeper into the workshop culture concept and explore how it takes workshops one step further.

Let's revisit the definition:

> Workshop culture = a team culture that uses the principles and practices of workshops and facilitation to encourage creativity and productivity, and to build the environment for effective collaboration.

By the end of this chapter, you will have learnt:

- why we need to think beyond the end of a workshop to make real impact in our work
- how to manage the seemingly opposing forces of ideation and execution
- the stages your team will progress through to transition to a workshop culture
- how design can help us to manage group dynamics, support progress and create connection.

The four foundations of a workshop culture

A workshop culture is just as much about mindset and approach as it is the practical elements of working together. A workshop culture has four core foundations:

1. Workshops are more than a one-off event.
2. Maintain a constant balance between creativity and productivity.
3. Make tiny tweaks, not sweeping changes.
4. A workshop culture is designed.

Foundation 1: workshops are more than a one-off event

The time

The first foundation of a workshop culture is that workshops and their principles should have a longer-term impact than just on the workshop day itself. A workshop is a specific period of time where people get together to discuss and explore a topic. There is a start and an end to the event.

Whether this workshop is run in-person or virtually, this time is marked as different to the everyday routine. A workshop is blocked out in a team's calendar, and they are expected to give their full focus during this time. Ideally, it's not something from which they can come and go. This carved out time prepares them to act and think differently than they would in their usual busy working days and meetings. There is also an expense attached, whether that is for travel and refreshments, booking a room or an external facilitator. The time needs to be well spent to justify the cost.

When we're building a workshop culture, this different way of thinking becomes a regular way of being in the team. It may still be necessary to allocate time for specific discussions, but these are no longer special and one-off occasions.

The space and set-up

When you walk into a room for an in-person workshop, you instantly know it's not business-as-usual. The chairs and tables are laid out differently. You'll see packs of sticky notes and markers, and flip charts. All this indicates that, in this space, you'll be working differently. Teams often value getting away from the office into a hired space to switch up their environment. These spaces might have quirky, creative decor and high ceilings, which encourage people to express more creativity, feel free to experiment and share thoughts that they might not usually share. When workshops are run virtually, this space is recreated through online whiteboards and interactive tools. Having these digital spaces displayed on the screen provides a similar signal to being in a different room – 'we are here to think differently. It's time to roll up our sleeves and get creative'.

For many, this workshop 'space' is seen as separate to their work – a time when they have permission to get messy. In a workshop culture, these spaces become more normalized into the everyday so that they merge with daily work.

The people and relationships

You are encouraged to be more relaxed in workshops than you might usually be at work, especially if you work in a more typically formal or corporate environment. With the help of a good facilitator, you can open up more than you would in a formal setting. A workshop format and setting seems to help people to do this, likely because of all the things I've already described. The facilitated conversations go deeper than the usual surface-based, task-focused discussions that drive work forward in a usual day. The facilitator creates more room for honesty and emotions by asking questions and encouraging the team to slow down, so there is more room for real connection and getting to know each other. As a result, workshops can be cathartic and a real space to take a deep breath and get a sense of enjoyment in our work.

In a workshop culture, this open communication is a natural feature. The real cohesion between team members enables them to share, honestly and openly, because of the supportive, collaborative environment that has been built.

REFLECTION: what happens after your workshops

- Does your organization allocate time to collaborative team sessions?
- If so, what happens when the workshop finishes? Is it back to business-as-usual?
- Where could workshops and their principles make a difference to the way that you work together?

Foundation 2: maintain a constant balance between creativity and productivity

The conflict between creativity and productivity

Workshops are sometimes criticized because it can be difficult to translate the ideas that have been generated into measurable actions with business value. When there is a separation between what happens in workshops and what might be seen as 'real work', it amounts to a conflict between creativity and execution, and being able to effectively balance them.

Workshops are associated with ideation and brainstorming – a non-linear activity without any guarantee of success. On the surface this can look inefficient, and so it feels easier to contain the process within a distinct time and space. Rather this than incorporate it into the rest of the organization, where it is hard to manage and measure.

'Real work' is often equated with task delivery. The more you complete, the more productive you are, which has a very direct impact on business bottom line. This may be based on previously proven results, and the aim is to be able to do the same task more efficiently and quickly over time.

Creativity and productivity often seem to be at odds with each other. Teresa Amabile has been studying creativity within organizations and teams throughout her academic career. In her early research, she recognized the challenge that companies have with maintaining creativity as they grow.[1] The drive towards efficiency favours task-driven execution over expansive, exploratory thinking, because the latter has no clear boundaries and so can be hard to justify.

While these processes might seem like opposites, when we look at them as connected, we see that they are fundamental to each other and are two parts of a bigger process. In a workshop culture, it's not about championing one or the other, but harnessing them both together. We start to see how investing in the seemingly chaotic creative process eventually contributes to better implementation, and how introducing some structure to idea generation can support progress.

Creating the space to be creative – fighting the illusion of 'inefficiency'

Uncertainty is a tricky thing to handle when you're trying to sustain and grow an organization, and so perhaps it feels easier to confine creativity to workshops. But to do this would be to miss out on the magic that creativity can bring to the everyday. We can't just tell people to 'go and be creative'. For creativity to work and have true value within a business, leaders need to deeply understand it and facilitate it in a way that can have real benefits for a team. This is where a workshop culture can help.

The skills needed to manage team creativity are very similar to workshop facilitation skills. Creativity needs careful handling to flourish. It doesn't thrive with micromanagement or command-and-control, but it does need guardrails. People can be their most creative when they have the freedom and flexibility to find their own way to solutions, and this is balanced with a framework or guidance. This might be a well-crafted open-ended question, a clear brief, a deadline or budget to work to, or other parameters that can focus idea generation. The solutions might not come immediately, but we need to trust that, through the process, they will. Guiding a team through this ambiguity is an essential part of making progress.

In fact, a workshop is not only about generating ideas, even though with all the sticky notes it may seem that way. A well-designed workshop swings between exploration and focus, divergent and convergent thinking, and moves participants through a narrative to generate and explore ideas, make them tangible and move forward.

A workshop culture encourages people to express creativity in their everyday role, not just in a dedicated brainstorming session. Within the context of the business, you start to sense when it's time to develop ideas and when it's time to act on them. You create the right balance, understanding the value that both ideas and execution bring, and are able to manage that delicate dance between the two.

A workshop culture doesn't make the workshop format redundant. There is still a lot of value in those intense working sessions where your team can centre in on a challenge. But a workshop shouldn't be the only place that you and your team feel like you can be creative, especially not for the sake of efficiency.

Leading teams through change

Workshops provide us with experience of how to operate and work together when we are moving through new challenges together and are tasked with innovation. We learn a lot about how to lead ourselves and our colleagues through the unknown.

A workshop culture helps our modern organizations build up tolerance for dealing with uncertainty. The creative process can be frustrating, uncomfortable and unpredictable, and we need to learn to stay with it as it develops into something useful. This exact scenario plays out in workshops when teams get stuck or feel unsure about next steps. The facilitator must be comfortable with this uncomfortable feeling – and maybe even welcome it!

At the same time, we need to be able to see through the chaos and make sense of it to make progress. A facilitator needs to reassure the team that what they are experiencing is normal, and guide them until they reach a point of clarity.

Foundation 3: make tiny tweaks, not sweeping changes

Change your approach to change

A workshop culture has an iterative and evolving nature, and it's also best introduced to a team in this way. Building a workshop culture is not a one-time event. It's a gradual shift in mindset and behaviour that comes about through small, regular tweaks.

Bringing more collaboration to your company doesn't have to start with a sweeping, widespread, top-level change. Long-term, sustainable culture change happens gradually, trickling through a company. Those leading the change gather individuals and teams along the journey, and together they create enduring habits and behaviours. It doesn't happen instantly. It's about starting with small wins, showing the impact they have and bringing people into a movement.

While it's not possible to completely change a team's culture in one workshop, it is often the start of the process. A fantastic workshop can kickstart the momentum that eventually leads to widespread company culture change. And once you run that first workshop, this is what the progress might look like for your team until you reach a fully fledged workshop culture:

1. Running one-off workshops
2. Having more regular workshops
3. Workshop culture.

Figure 3.1 Stages to achieving a fully fledged workshop culture.

1. Running one-off workshops

A team's first experience of a workshop with a professional facilitator can be transformative. Their point of reference is often the many unproductive meetings they've attended. Many people are amazed by the effectiveness of the format: how much they get done within a short space of time and the insights they gain. The workshop has demonstrated how a different way of working is possible.

When this happens, it's important to reinforce the next steps after the workshop – ensuring the team remains aligned, that they have clarity, that they act upon their ideas and incorporate them into their work.

The team has had a positive experience and has been converted to the power of workshops. But as we know by now, this is just the start.

2. Having more regular workshops

The next stage is making workshops a more regular feature of work. A team may be familiar and comfortable with the format, but up until this point, workshops are still seen as relatively separate from their everyday work. For example, they may run workshops to support an innovative side project, or to run idea-generation sessions or project retrospectives. In this way, workshops remain very much as defined events, but teams are able to transition into 'workshop mode' more fluidly.

As teams become increasingly familiar with the format, they may start to bring elements of workshops into their regular meetings – for example, having a quick, facilitated brainstorm or recording notes visually. It's easier to introduce these methods, because the team has already been oriented to them. The team has recognized the value of using workshop techniques to improve their meetings and achieve better outcomes.

When a team starts to work like this, they clearly see the difference between an ineffective meeting and a great workshop, and want to continue making the most of the time they spend together. They see that this benefits how they work as a team overall, and they can see the value of facilitation.

3. Workshop culture

A team reaches a fully fledged workshop culture when they have progressed through stages one and two, and markedly transformed the way they work together. They form new habits and ways of interacting inspired by workshop techniques and principles. They have richer conversations, ask more questions and listen to each other more intently. Team members take more ownership to improve the way they work together, because they are empowered to initiate change, no matter their position or level. It becomes an integral part of their attitude to work. Essentially, the behaviours they display in a workshop become how they behave as a team.

Of course, progressing through these three stages is not quite as linear as I have illustrated. It is an iterative process. Transitioning to a workshop culture doesn't happen immediately, and there is no specified time for how long it takes to progress through the stages. This depends on the team and their context. Sometimes it simply takes a while for a team to see opportunities to run more workshops. In any case, they must gradually adjust to engaging with each other differently. Any attempt to suddenly force a team to work in a new way will likely result in resistance.

But what does happen is that little shifts start to make a big impact. For example, as meetings are such a painful experience for many people, when they are introduced to a method that can save them time, or that can help them increase the quality of their work and make their working lives better, they are often eager to try it.

We explore tactics for initiating and sustaining change in Chapter 9.

REFLECTION: change

Where do you see opportunities to make small shifts to improve the way you work together?

Foundation 4: a workshop culture is designed

The importance of intention

Like a great workshop, a workshop culture is *designed*. To build all of the factors we explored in Chapter 2 (true collaboration, facilitation, curiosity, etc.), you will need to intentionally create the conditions for them. A workshop facilitator doesn't just turn up on the day of the session without preparation, hoping that everything will fall into place. They deliberately craft an outline for the outcomes they need to achieve and the environment they want to create. They consider what needs to be discussed, who will be in the session and how they might interact with each other. Then they design a workshop that they believe will get them to where they want to be.

We need to take this same approach to our team cultures – consciously designing how we work. A new challenge gives us an opportunity to be thoughtful about how we will address it. A new team enables us to review the value each individual brings and the reason we brought everyone together. A workshop culture appreciates that there is no one size fits all, and that we need to consider people and the context. Depending on who we're working with, we can craft a unique experience based on how we will best collaborate. Then, we use all of the elements of workshops, in particular facilitation, to guide us through doing that great work.

Designing for group dynamics

Group dynamics cover a broad area, defined by the American Psychological Association as 'the processes, operations, and changes that occur within social groups, which affect patterns of affiliation, communication, conflict, conformity, decision-making, influence, leadership, norm formation, and power.'[2] Within the context of our teams, group dynamics can be tricky to navigate, and there are a number of common traps to be aware of. For example, there may be team members that dominate the discussion in meetings. These could be people that have been in the team longer, are more senior or are more extraverted. Whatever their position, they are the ones that feel more comfortable to speak up. They may have valuable contributions to make, but it means that more introverted, less confident or junior members of the team do not participate as much. The impact is that those that talk the most seem to be the only ones with ideas. One of the most important roles a facilitator can have is to bring those quieter voices into the foreground to demonstrate that great ideas can come from anywhere.

In addition, carefully crafting a group of team members with diverse characteristics doesn't automatically mean the conversation will be full of wonderfully diverse opinions. As we've explored in Chapter 2, many people will avoid conflict and do not like openly disagreeing with each other. If your team looks harmonious on the surface, you may have fallen into the 'groupthink' trap. Groupthink is the tendency for people to agree in order to keep the peace or to avoid being disruptive. When this happens, your team is far from fulfilling their potential, because they are not pushing themselves past what feels comfortable. They are not benefiting from the rich, dynamic clash of ideas that leads to innovation. Facilitators know how to introduce challenge to a group so that they can combat the natural dynamics that might occur.

You may be aware of the various dynamics that exist in your team, and know that they can do great harm to collaboration, but are unsure of how to address them. Facilitators do their best before a workshop to consider the group they will be working with and design activities to combat these tendencies. They will also be on constant lookout during a session for these dynamics. This may be, for example, alternating between full group discussions and smaller breakout groups in meetings, allowing for individual reflection, or even considering how to use tools like sticky notes or online whiteboards to ensure everyone has a chance to share their thoughts.

We want the most fertile environment for creativity and equal contributions. If we can create activities in workshops to optimize performance, we can do the same with our teamwork. I'll share more about meeting dynamics in Chapter 7.

Designing for progress

When a team commits to a workshop, it's because they want to move something forward – a project, an initiative, an idea, a plan – and they know that if they didn't dedicate this time and energy, it wouldn't get the same attention. A workshop also enables a team to openly explore all the factors that are preventing them from moving forward, so that they can agree on practical actions to overcome those factors.

A workshop outline is a narrative that takes a team on a journey towards an end goal. A facilitator considers what a team needs to discuss and explore, and arranges it together in a logical order for them to address. They will look at the potential roadblocks, and design activities to help a team break through them. In a workshop culture, we see challenges not as dead ends but as opportunities to design a new way of working together to take a team to the next level.

Most new plans and ideas are likely to come up against blockers. As a team, your work will have its own challenges. You will also be operating within a context and environment that are part of a larger system, often out of your control. You may experience challenges in interacting with other stakeholders, systems that slow you down, or have budget or resource constraints. These factors could become real barriers to getting work done. Making progress isn't about avoiding them entirely; it's about having strategies to address them when they come up. If you fully recognize what could get in the way of your team moving forward, design with this in mind, and even celebrate these factors as what makes your culture unique. They can be the defining events that help your team to perform above and beyond.

Designing for connection

Workshops and a workshop culture are powerful when the people working within them have an opportunity to build an authentic connection.

In a task-driven world, we focus on getting things done and checking items off of our to-do lists. But we also need to create the glue that brings people together and makes our collaborative tasks so much easier. If not, we risk being highly transactional in our meetings. They can simply be seen as a method of getting through a list of points on an agenda. Meetings like this may be efficient, but they miss an important human element. When we have the time to slow down, pause and relate to each other, we bring a little warmth back to work. This is not forced connection, but enabling people to bring more of themselves, enough for people to get to know each other behind their jobs.

The MIT Human Dynamics Research Lab performed a study that demonstrated how the teams that engaged in informal, frequent communication were the ones that performed more highly. In one management study of a call centre, the introduction of a group break at the same time enabled the team to socialize and form connections. This resulted in an increase in productivity (measured by how quickly they were able to handle calls) and significant cost savings.[3] A workshop culture recognizes that the spaces in between the tasks are just as important as the tasks themselves, and that we need to intentionally create the space for these interactions to happen. They are not a secondary part or an added bonus of work; they are part of the work itself.

REFLECTION: designing your team

- Where in your team can you see that being more intentional in the way that you work together could make a difference?
- What are some of the group dynamics occurring in your team that you'd like to address?
- What barriers and blockers do you frequently experience in your team, and how could you consciously move through them or around them?
- How can you ensure that work goes beyond being transactional to building real connection between team members?

Chapter 3 – key takeaways:

- Our organizations favour productivity, but once we learn how to harness creativity effectively, we can see that they're both part of the same overall process.
- Workshops offer a peek into what it's like to lead teams through uncertainty – exactly what we need in our modern organizations.
- A workshop culture doesn't happen overnight; we gradually shift towards it by introducing the workshop format and new ways of meeting to our team.
- When we're more intentional and design how our team works together – looking at group dynamics and the specific challenges we face – we are more likely to make progress and build authentic connection.

Now that we've built up a picture of the nuts and bolts of a workshop culture, let's turn to you and what you need, as a leader, to start your team on this journey.

Chapter 4

Leading a workshop culture

A workshop culture starts with you. At the end of Chapter 1, we presented some different scenarios that you might be experiencing and your reason for implementing a workshop culture. Whatever your situation, you want to make change happen. If this sounds daunting, know that you don't need to start with big sweeping changes or an overhaul of everything you're currently doing. As we've just explored in Chapter 3, the smallest step forward can make a big difference.

That doesn't mean it will be easy. Building a workshop culture will require some shifts in your thinking, mindset and behaviour. As the one initiating the change, you will need some essential core skills. This chapter prepares you for the practical implementation that will come next. You'll get some insight into some foundations that will make the concept more real and, therefore, more learnable.

By the end of this chapter, you will have learnt how:

- a workshop culture is about balancing a range of different elements that are often in flux, and that there are core skills that will help you do this
- to transfer workshop facilitation skills to the process of leading a workshop culture
- to think strategically in terms of team culture development, and the value of making time for this activity.

CASE STUDY: the challenge of change

One of my clients found out how challenging the process of changing behaviour can be.

Louise (name changed) was one of the most powerful leaders I've worked with, respected for her business and executive experience in some of the world's leading creative technology companies. She was passionate about enabling people to be their best selves, but had inherited a team that was burned out, unhappy and stressed. She approached me to deliver a programme that would help undo some of the unproductive behaviours that had become embedded.

Louise had a vivid vision for a thriving, collaborative and supportive workplace, but her team hadn't experienced this kind of leadership before. They were not used to thinking about work as a place that could be nourishing and fulfilling. As much as Louise was driven to make work better for her colleagues, because of her positive outlook (who wouldn't want to create a happy working environment?) she underestimated how difficult it would be to bring people along on the journey. This was a big learning curve in her own personal and professional development.

First, we had to understand that nothing would happen overnight, and we would only see the change looking back over a period of time. We couldn't only expect to see this daily, or even weekly. It might even take a few months for some changes to really take hold.

Then we had to accept what was in our control and what wasn't. Some people had more work to do to build emotional intelligence, and we had to explore how to work with this, and at their speed, rather than constantly knocking at a door that wasn't ready to open.

This meant continuing the momentum with those that were positive about change, while working directly and sensitively with those that may have been unintentionally (or intentionally!) blocking progress.

We also had to be prepared for what I call 'the point of no return'. It's like clearing out a cupboard that you haven't attended to in years. The first bit is easy, as you're pulling everything out to see what's there and to create space. But when everything is out of the cupboard and piled in a big mess, you realize you've got a long way to go to reorganize it. It may feel like things are getting worse before they get better, but you can't turn back, as you've started the process. (I often encounter this in workshops too!)

Louise was determined and motivated. Over a six-month period, she attended every single team workshop to demonstrate that she was also learning and she and her team were all in the development together. She made sure that the team continued conversations outside of the programme about the actions they had committed to. It was a regular discussion point in their meetings. Louise integrated our work into other parts of her business planning. It was hard for her team to forget about it.

In our advisory sessions, I encouraged Louise to note down the small wins she was noticing each week. It might have been a small shift in an individual's behaviour, someone introducing a new idea to support the team, or a different energy in the meetings. It was important to see how this was all adding up to make a difference.

Louise didn't see the end of our engagement as the end of the transformation. Instead, her team of senior managers had started to bring more facilitation principles into their strategic planning and were creating a roadmap for how to continue the process of change with their direct reports.

The role of a change agent

When you've decided that you'd like to build a workshop culture, you've taken on the role of a change agent. You have taken on the responsibility of guiding the shifts that will bring out the best in your team. It also means you need to look at *change* in a different way.

We've all experienced a big change, like getting a new job or moving home. These big changes have a start, middle and end. There is a finality to what you want to happen, and you will know when you've got there.

When you are a change agent for a workshop culture, there won't be a point when you say 'we're done!' because you will be in a constant state of evolution. There will always be something to respond to, whether that's a new project, a business opportunity or even external societal shifts that you can't plan for. And so a workshop culture requires you to see change as a continuous process. You don't implement change and then end there; change is happening all the time.

This means developing a new mindset – one that allows you and your team to handle any disruption that comes your way. There is no finish line to cross, but more of a settling into and getting comfortable with ongoing flux. So yes, while this is all about changing your team's culture, ultimately the real transformation is in you and your colleagues. This is about altering the way you think and approach your work forever.

What you can control and what you can't

Before you set off on your journey of change, prepare yourself for what's to come. The role of the change agent can be frustrating and feel thankless if you don't take the right approach. In your journey, you will encounter people who have no desire to change, either through lack of awareness or pure stubbornness. They may fear the new or want to protect their own position. The existing culture, however toxic, may be comfortable to them because it's familiar and helps them to feel in control. There will be deep-rooted habits and behaviours that seem almost impossible to undo. In your wider organization, there may be entrenched systems and processes that could take months or even years to shift. Trying to change any of this head-on, and alone, will be an uphill battle. So it's important to start with some easy wins.

Begin with your vision of change (refer back to the reflection exercise in the introduction), and map out your lofty goals. Next, assess what is in your ability to change, and what isn't. Stand firmly in the former. Be honest about what you have a direct influence over and what you don't (in *The 7 Habits of Highly Effective People*, Stephen Covey suggests identifying what is your circle of control, circle of influence and circle of concern[1]). Then create a plan to get started with your first small step. A big wholesale change may initially feel exhilarating, but it will take a lot of effort, and you'll likely come up against so many barriers you will burnout before you've had the chance to make an impact. Start with where you can make an immediate shift, in a small way to start the momentum, and it will make your role as a change agent easier in the long run.

It's also worth remembering to be easy on yourself. Celebrate your small wins and track your progress, because in the short term the impact of the actions you're taking may seem imperceptible. However, when you look back over a longer period of time, you will see how far you and your team have come.

Your toolkit for introducing a workshop culture

As a change agent, in addition to the framework that we cover in Part 3, you will need a number of tools to introduce a workshop culture to your team. These tools will help you to lead your team effectively through the transformation. Figure 4.1 gives an overview of how you will need to balance thinking with doing and people with business.

Figure 4.1 Introducing a workshop culture:
balancing people with business and thinking with doing.

Let's start in the centre and work outwards:

- *Collaboration* is at the centre of the framework because it underpins everything we are doing. It's the driver for building a workshop culture.
- *Facilitation* is the natural way to support collaboration. This approach and the associated skills are essential.

Strategic thinking and *design mindset* are about imagining and creating what's possible. They are about building ideas for what and how you want your team to be.

- *Strategic thinking* sets the north star. It provides a long-term direction. Without it, it's difficult to stay committed to building a workshop culture. The results aren't always immediate, and the short term can be more seductive and urgent to address. So it's always vital to keep one foot in the future, while responding to what is needed at the present time.

- *Design mindset* is about taking an intentional approach to teamwork. Understanding that great teams do not just happen by themselves, and the chances of success are greatly increased by designing the way you work.

Behaviour change and *ideas to action* are about making it all happen in practice.

- *Ideas to action* is the ability to move from the abstract to the practical, and in translating broad concepts, like a strategic direction, into the clear action steps that will make goals happen. This is on the 'business side' of the framework because it helps us to make the connection between a future goal and what you need to start doing now to get there.
- *Behaviour change* is the awareness of how to shift habits and ways of doing. Setting an intention doesn't always mean that we will take the necessary action. Behaviour change is about having a deep understanding of and a curiosity for how we, as human beings, are motivated to change. Behaviour change sits on the 'people' side of the framework as you take your team through from creating a new way of working to implementing it in practice.

Monitoring the balance between all of these areas will lead to a strong workshop culture. That balance will be ever-shifting and changing as your team evolves, and you will be regularly tweaking the levels to get the optimum output at a particular time. We'll now dig into each of these elements in turn.

Collaboration: a collaboration mindset

Building a workshop culture starts with truly believing that others have valuable insights and knowledge to share, and having a genuine curiosity for their opinions. Prepare yourself to be surprised, and delighted, by what happens when you open up the floor for others to contribute. In a world where leaders are expected to have all the answers, this can be challenging. It can be a big step to take.

It can feel unnatural, or even vulnerable to move into a space where you admit you 'don't know', especially in a culture where we are promoted upwards based on our individual performance, technical expertise and ability to make decisions. But one person in a team cannot know all the solutions to the challenges that a team needs to solve, especially in the uncertain world we are in. And so we need to be willing to bring other people into the conversation. We need to start asking more questions rather than only giving answers. Without this shift, any effort to implement a workshop culture will not work.

The hard work of soft skills

This shift may require getting familiar with some different emotions and new interpersonal skills. Building a workshop culture is a very people-based endeavour, and it's impossible to avoid addressing the human element that comes with this. Here are some examples:

Letting go of control

Accepting that you will no longer be able to predict or control the outcome of your team. You will only be able to put the foundations in place for your team to get to the best outcome themselves. It's a balance between providing a scaffold, and then allowing your team to use that structure in the way that works for them.

Trust

Having the confidence in your team's ability and ensuring they know that they are trusted. Although this is important for the work your team produces, it also has another outcome – ensuring people are invested in, and take ownership for, their own work.

Handling uncertainty

When your team faces a new challenge, you won't know the answers immediately. Instead, you'll be in an ongoing cycle of problem-solving. Sitting with this uncertainty is something we need to practice. It's the very reason we need effective collaboration.

Openness

True collaboration is impossible to achieve if the motivation does not come from a genuine desire to know what other people think. Workshop culture will mean hearing from more voices. Inviting people in can be messy (and so uncertainty pops up again!) – we don't know what they're going to say or how they will respond.

At the same time, if you're leading a workshop culture, you will need to lead by example by being more open about your own insights, thought processes, plans and even challenges so that people have the information they need to operate effectively.

Vulnerability

A workshop culture takes a lot of experimentation and the willingness to try something new. You will make mistakes, and not all plans will work out. Owning this vulnerable position is powerful and sets your team up to have more connected and authentic conversations.

These are some of the key factors that are often holding us back from true collaboration. Collaboration is a skill. It may feel uncomfortable and awkward at first, but it becomes more familiar (but not necessarily easier!) with time. These skills are essential for workshop facilitators and those leading a workshop culture.

For now, reflect on how some of those areas sit with you.

REFLECTION: are you ready to collaborate?

To assess your attitude to true collaboration, rate yourself on the following statements on a scale of 1–5, where 1 is not at all and 5 is fully ready.

> I truly believe that collaboration is the best way of getting things done in my company (not because I've been told to or can't avoid it).

> I am interested to hear what others' opinions are, even if they differ from my own.

> I am prepared to have my ideas challenged, even by people that are not as experienced as me.

> I am prepared to see what emerges in a project rather than having everything planned out according to what has worked for me in the past.

> I am prepared to try new ways of working and to let things work out differently from what I planned.

> I am ready to let go of tasks and responsibilities that have previously been in my control.

> I trust that if I give more autonomy and freedom to my team, they will do a good job.

> I do not need to have a complete handle on everything for it to go well.

> I am ready to open up various aspects of my work for input from others.

> I am ready to respond with 'I don't know' when someone asks me a question.

TRY THIS: build collaboration capacity

One way to start building your capacity for collaboration is to open up a small part of your work for input from your team. Make sure it's low stakes for you, until you build more confidence, and craft some good open-ended questions that would help you fill some of your gaps in knowledge. For example:

- What might I be missing here?
- How could I make this better?
- If you were working on this, what would you do next?

See what happens, not only for the responses you get, but for how your team responds to you asking for their input.

Facilitation: there's something about facilitation

In Chapter 2, we described facilitation as a feature of a great workshop and the role of a workshop facilitator. Here we'll focus on how it applies in your capacity for leading a workshop culture.

Concepts like intrinsic motivation, flexibility and the right amount of challenge have all been identified as factors that support and encourage creativity.[2] This makes sense. When bringing together people because of their skills and expertise, why would we direct and limit how they work? Instead, it's more about guiding their talents towards an outcome, creating the conditions for them to do their work to the best of their ability and removing any barriers that might get in the way. The key to that is 'facilitation' rather than 'management'.

The fact that a workshop facilitator is often not a subject-matter expert can be a huge advantage. They are there to make sure the discussion stays productive and on track, and that everyone gets involved and shares their knowledge. A facilitator needs to stay objective – enough to spot any dynamics that can thwart the good efforts of the team. They take an impartial position and remember the overall higher-level purpose of the workshop when the group is deep in discussion or getting lost in detail.

Taking this approach as a leader has an impact on both how a team performs together and business performance. Carmeli and Paulus discovered that CEOs are able to generate more knowledge sharing and creativity in their top management teams when they have a specific skill called 'ideational facilitation leadership'.[3] They described how having this exploratory and problem-solving mindset is necessary for introducing new ideas that might lead to innovation.

Facilitation applied to a workshop culture

In a workshop culture, facilitation is needed both to generate content and to develop process:

1. The workshops you run with your team to get work done – content-focused

In a workshop culture, some of your regular meetings will transform into workshop-style sessions that are more interactive and inclusive. These sessions may be directly related to generating content, such as brainstorming, project kick-offs or planning sessions. These content-focused workshops create information and ideas that form the substance of your work.

2. The workshops you run with your team to enhance and support your culture – process-focused

Process-focused workshops help your team to explore the way you work together, the habits you build as a team and your general culture. Creating a workshop culture is a collaborative process, and you will be supporting your team to co-design the way that they work. The outputs from these sessions will not be visible in the work your team produces, but they will guide how you get it done.

You will begin to find that facilitation and its principles will start to seep into every aspect of the way your team interacts. You will find evidence of workshop culture everywhere, not just in your meetings. It will be present in the way you talk to each other, the systems you set up to communicate and maybe even what your workspace looks like. A workshop culture is sustained when it is embedded in this way.

You may find that you build the mindset for collaboration and then bring more facilitation techniques into your meetings as a natural extension of this. Or you may start running workshop-style meetings and introduce those principles slowly, which in turn changes your attitude towards work. Either way, breaking down the skills of running workshops starts to make the abstract concept of collaboration more real and practical.

How to become a good facilitator

Facilitation can seem like a mystical skill. Many who are new to it are daunted by it. It's not like public speaking, where you can rehearse your talk over and over again before performing the real thing. The only way to truly practice facilitation is to do it live, which means on-the-job, in-front-of-everyone training. The biggest and most important variable is how workshop participants react. This is impossible to predict and feels risky, especially as it's their responses that determine the success of a session.

So, frustratingly, the best approach is to accept that you have no control over what will happen, yet plan as though you will. This means having the best intentions for the session, such as a clear purpose, structured timing, desired outcomes and ensuring that you have considered dynamics, but holding the workshop outline lightly and being prepared to switch things around if necessary.

This balance of intention and flexibility is also central to a workshop culture. We start off with a plan, which sets us off in the right direction, but as we learn more, we shift and evolve while still keeping an eye on what we want to achieve. If that needs to change too, then we can adjust our end goal accordingly. Ironically, this openness and willingness to change helps us prepare for what we can't prepare for!

Key skills for facilitation

Facilitation involves a number of skills which include reading the room, keeping up energy and capturing content. Many of these must be practised during a workshop, but there are some foundational skills that you can develop outside of a group setting. This helps to create familiarity when you need them during a session.

Be more curious

As we covered in Chapter 2, curiosity is fast becoming an essential skill for the business of the future. With so many new challenges constantly arising, it's not just about searching for novel solutions, it's about searching for the right problem in the first place. Here, the key facilitation skill of asking great, genuinely curious questions takes centre stage. Instead of providing answers, a facilitator asks the right questions that spark thinking and discussion. In *Humble Inquiry: The Gentle Art of Asking Instead of Telling*, Edgar Schein explains how learning to ask better questions is key to building relationships in a collaborative workplace. He defines 'humble inquiry' as 'the fine art of drawing someone out, of asking questions to which you do not already know the answer, of building a relationship based on curiosity and interest in the other person'.[4]

Consider where in your work and everyday conversations you can practice creating more open-ended queries for your team to get them thinking and building connection.

Become a better listener

After asking questions, a facilitator says very little. Instead they listen intently to what is being said and also what is *not* being said (i.e. body language, energy of the group and other subtle reactions), so that they can ask more questions. Good listening is needed to capture content, but also to notice what is happening within the group's dynamics.

Where in your work can you observe more and listen to get a sense of the dynamics?

Practice empathy

Facilitation is not just about dealing with content that the participants generate, but the possible tensions that come with it. Sometimes, ideas and opinions are loaded with history and emotions, so may require deeper enquiry to move through them. While it's easy to label someone as 'difficult' for blocking or preventing progress, facilitation requires understanding that there may be a reason behind someone's defensive behaviour. Facilitation requires directness that is delivered with tact and sensitivity.

Consider some of the challenging relationships you have in your work. How could you understand more about the other person's perspective? We delve more into building empathy in Chapter 6.

Learn to synthesize

When you have created a more open and inclusive environment through asking questions and better listening, you've opened up the potential for more perspectives to surface. There will be both aligning and conflicting viewpoints. A facilitator must be able to handle multiple perspectives and help participants to make sense of this complexity. This is one of the advantages of staying objective. With a little distance from the discussion, a facilitator is able to create simplicity out of the chaos, draw out key points and reflect back to the participants to build clarity.

When you find yourself as part of a complex discussion, pause and take a step back to see if you can spot any connections and insights that you may have previously missed.

Cultivate patience and persistence

Facilitation, although hugely rewarding, is also challenging work. Not everything a facilitator does is visible, and you use a lot of mental energy. What should my next question be? Is everyone contributing? What is not being said? Are we on track to achieve our goals? Dealing with the creative process, chaos and uncertainty is unsettling. It can feel easier to revert to our comfortable position of directing and giving our opinions rather than holding back and knowing that a team can work it out themselves. Facilitation requires patience and emotional intelligence that grounds you when everything seems to be up in the air.

When someone on your team approaches you with a challenge they are experiencing, consider how you can take a bit more time to help them find a solution themselves rather than providing your own, even if you're certain you are right and it would take less time.

Meetings and facilitation form a large part of the Communication pillar for workshop culture, which we cover in Chapter 7.

Strategic thinking: important, but not urgent

When we're overwhelmed with work, we naturally focus on what is most urgent. We need tasks to be delivered faster and to get more done in less time. We need results on a timeline of days and weeks (maybe even hours!), not months and years, and so our pressing tasks demand more of our attention. It's easy to get seduced by the to-dos that are shouting the loudest, but this creates a bias towards short-term results, and can eventually have consequences for us and our team.

When we prioritize the short term, we become mainly concerned with what can be delivered quickly, regardless of how it fits into the overall, wider scope of what our team needs to achieve. Work becomes disconnected, and we start to create silos. The long-term impact of those immediate actions has not been considered, and it can lead to confusion and duplication.

The Eisenhower Matrix, a popular tool used for time management, illustrates this challenge well. It categorizes tasks into four areas depending on whether they are urgent or not urgent, important or not important. Naturally, we're drawn to focusing on our urgent tasks even if they are not important, and it's the 'important but not urgent' tasks that suffer.

So we need to:

1. address the urgent and important tasks first
2. delegate the urgent tasks that are not important
3. eliminate the tasks that are neither urgent nor important
4. plan time to focus on what's important but not urgent.

Strategic thinking is one of those 'important but not urgent' tasks that we must make room for in our schedules. It means thinking broadly about the future and the bigger picture, not just what is in our current line of vision.

Because it is less visible and real and not something we need to do 'right now', it can be hard to justify allocating time and resources to strategic thinking. In fact, it can feel like a luxury. But with the majority of leaders – 97% – believing that strategic thinking is vital to organizational success,[5] carving out the time for you and your team to think strategically is a necessity. This is the case even if it does seem like an act of bravery in a busy world that favours rapid results.

Why we need strategic thinking

Connecting the dots at the daily level

While you may be productive without thinking about the bigger picture, you may be working on the wrong things. Strategic thinking is about taking time to step back to look holistically at your work. A strategic outlook makes sure that the dots are connected at the daily level and you're moving forward in the right direction. This helps to guide your daily decision-making to be more focused and deliberate rather than ad hoc or scattered, and it will all be aligned to the longer-term goal.

You get better ideas

Thinking strategically enables you to be more ambitious as a team. You're able to pool your resources and set goals that you can only achieve together with this unique group of people. Strategic thinking means bringing in high-level knowledge in response to a challenge and creating your specific approach based on the collective intelligence of your team.

It promotes collaboration

It's difficult to see the importance of teamwork when you only have a myopic view of your own area and contribution. When your team can see that the end goal can only be achieved through great collaboration, they will be more motivated to work through challenges, with the recognition that you are all 'in it together'. Having a sense of the bigger picture enables your team to stay connected and focused on the purpose. We've already explored how important purpose is in Chapter 1, and we'll look at it again in Chapter 5, which covers the first pillar of the framework for building a workshop culture – Alignment.

Strategic thinking is a creative task – here's how to do it

Strategic thinking is initially a creative task, and it takes imagination, visioning and positivity before you move into the pragmatic phase of implementation. You're thinking about the potential of what could happen, and by doing that you're creating a path and a direction in which to move. There are no initial right answers to strategic thinking. You're making bets based on knowledge, experience and some historic data of where you should be heading.

With technical expertise, you need to go deep to develop your craft. The deeper you go, the better you become, and it leads to specialization. By contrast, strategic thinking pushes you in the other direction – away from the detail into a more general and high-level space. You want to consider a range of topics, not laser focus on one area.

Strategic thinking comes with an inherent curiosity and even a sense of wonder for seeing the larger system within which you work. There is a desire to understand wider patterns and trends to form an overview. Good strategic thinkers are able to handle the range of viewpoints, angles and opinions that come from their team and other stakeholders.

Strategic thinking – where and when

Strategic thinking requires a different headspace to your regular thinking. It's near impossible to engage in a task like this when you're buried in an ongoing cycle of to-dos. It works well to carve out time, and possibly to change your environment. This can often happen more effectively outside of the usual physical space you work in, in an environment designed to promote creative thinking. For example, research has demonstrated that rooms with high ceilings create feelings of freedom and can prime our thinking in this way.[6]

Strategic thinking is not something that is just done once at the start of the year – it's something to come back to regularly. You will need to check the relevance of your ideas and adapt based on what might have changed. Your broad goal needs to stay flexible while you keep checking that you're on the right path or if you need to change direction. Like a workshop outline, you need to hold your ideas loosely because once they hit the real world, they may change in ways that you hadn't predicted.

A workshop culture requires us to be strategic thinkers so that we can reinforce a strong, compelling rationale for collaboration.

Design mindset: designing for culture change

In Chapter 2, I introduced how design thinking techniques can help our teams to improve communication. More generally, a 'design mindset' can also help us to look differently at our culture and teams. We can design how we work together, for a specific outcome, and use design methodologies to come up with innovative ways to collaborate.

In 2003, the Design Council, a UK-based organization advocating for the value of design in business, synthesized the process into the 'Double Diamond', shown in Figure 4.2.[7] This has now become a widely recognized and referenced model. The Double Diamond encourages us to find the right problem before we start creating solutions. We ask questions through a *discovery* process to get to the heart of a challenge or opportunity before going on to *define* the problem statement that we will work on as a team. Once the challenge is clearly defined, we *develop* a range of potential solutions, not to find the one right answer, but to brainstorm possibilities. Finally we converge on a solution to *deliver* and implement, not as the ultimate final stage but more as a prototype, which we will then use to gather more data and information about what might work in the real world.

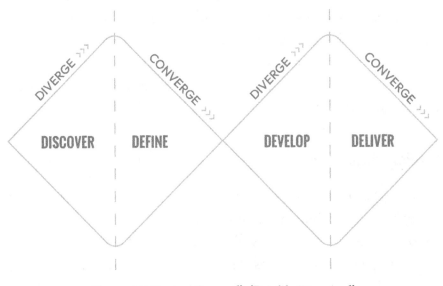

Figure 4.2 Design Council's 'Double Diamond'.
Reproduced with permission.

This approach is not something we traditionally associate with teamwork and collaboration. We might give this time, space and thinking to products and services, but not for how we work together. This is where there is great potential. We look at applying design to your teamwork more in Chapter 8.

Designing our work

There is no universal way of working that fits every team or organization. A design mindset puts you and your team at the centre of your working experience. You problem-solve and co-create to build the right methods for your team. You'll use skills like curiosity, exploration, experimentation and empathy to create what you believe will work for your team within your context.

When we realize we have agency over our working methods, both individually and collectively, it gives us a new outlook. We may have mostly been leaving this as an afterthought, focusing more on the content we produce and *what* we're doing to do. The recognition that it is possible to design *how* we work shows us that we have more influence and autonomy than we think. This realization alone can start to change our relationship with our jobs, and this has an amazing potential for the workplace.

Turning ideas to action

Creating the right conditions for great ideas to emerge freely, either through strategic thinking or otherwise, is just the first (albeit an important) step of building a workshop culture. It then becomes about supporting your team to translate those concepts and early ideas into action and maintain the momentum that keeps everyone engaged.

While you need to have sensitivity towards the creative process and let ideas breathe, you also need a bias towards action. This involves breaking big concepts into smaller parts, making ideas visible and real. It's a true art to manage this balance and shift from thinking into doing.

When you realize your team has a wealth of ideas that simply need to be surfaced, you'll see how it's not generating ideas that's the challenge, it's making them happen. This was explored by Scott Belsky in his book *Making Ideas Happen: Overcoming the Obstacles Between Vision and Reality*, which covered that the main challenges are factors such as organizational capability, leadership skill and momentum, rather than the quality of the ideas themselves.[8] To reduce the gap between ideas and action, ask yourself questions such as: how are people going to integrate a new idea practically into their daily work? How will they fit it in amongst all of their existing work? What do they need to reframe to make this action relevant for them? What new behaviours do they need to adopt to implement these new ideas?

Behaviour change

Whenever we want to achieve something that we haven't before, it means acting in a new way, too. When we are able to allocate the time, generating ideas is relatively easy in comparison to executing them. There are things we say we want to do, but in practice it is much harder.

This is what can let a great workshop down. Even if the experience of the session is fantastic, it's just the start. A workshop becomes more impactful if it effects real change afterwards. And this is why a facilitator also considers what will happen after the workshop. They will thoughtfully create exercises that nudge people towards their own ways of adopting change. The follow-up is where the next phase of work begins. This is where people will have to change established habits, overcome their own resistance and stay motivated to keep going.

Understanding what motivates people to change their behaviour is useful in your role as a change agent. Yet remember that this is a co-design process. Your team has to collectively drive this change. It ultimately comes from them in the pursuit of a happier, engaging and more productive working environment.

If you can run great workshops, you can implement a workshop culture

You're already ready

The process of starting to build a workshop culture is so similar to the process of designing and facilitating a workshop (which is of course the premise of this book) that if you are doing this effectively, you already have many of the skills you need (and if you're not, it's possible for you to quickly get up to speed). Referring again to Figure 4.1, showing what's needed to balance people with business and thinking with doing, here's a quick review of how the skills overlap.

Authentic workshops have collaboration at their core, achieved through facilitation. An effective workshop has the long term in mind, considering what happens beyond the end of the session. It puts the participant at the centre of the experience. When running a workshop, there must be a balance between what the business needs and creating an environment to get the best out of the individuals attending. And finally, the trickiest parts of the workshop process are: (1) turning all of the ideas generated into actions and (2) ensuring that the necessary behaviour change happens afterwards.

An effective workshop has three stages:

- Before the event (design) – understanding the purpose of the workshop and designing the right process to match.
- During the event (facilitation) – using facilitation skills to guide participants through activities and making sure everyone contributes.
- After the event (follow-up) – translating the outcomes and content from the workshop into the day-to-day.

These elements are all found in building a workshop culture except that instead of distinct periods before, during and after an event, as we see in a workshop, these steps may be less defined, non-linear and ubiquitous. Nevertheless, as Figure 4.3 shows, the skills used in each of these stages are completely transferable from workshop to workshop culture if we look at it as: (1) preparing for a workshop culture, (2) guiding a team through a workshop culture and (3) embedding a workshop culture.

	Running a workshop	Building a workshop culture
Before / preparing	Knowing a workshop is the right approach because you want to bring people together to work collaboratively. Thinking of the long-term impact of the workshop.	Having a real reason and drive to implement a workshop culture. Looking at the bigger picture and understanding how the parts fit together.
During / guiding	Using facilitation skills to guide participants through activities and make sure everyone contributes.	Using facilitation skills to encourage inclusivity, participation and engagement.
After / embedding	Translating the outcomes and content from the workshop into the day-to-day.	Understanding how to shift behaviour, and bring people on the journey.

Figure 4.3 The transferable skills from running a workshop to building a workshop culture.

Preparing for a workshop culture

The very first step in introducing a workshop culture is having the right motivation. In particular, you need a strong belief in collaboration and that striving to work together more effectively is really the best approach. Building a workshop culture is also thinking about the bigger picture and having a clear purpose. Although it's rewarding, changing culture is challenging and so requires a strong commitment to be able to stick with the process for the long term.

Guiding your team through a workshop culture

There is no end point to a workshop culture as there is with a workshop, but moving a team through it is heavily based on using facilitation to encourage inclusivity, participation and engagement. This needs the right skills to guide your team through the process, rather than direct them, and bring out the best in people.

Embedding a workshop culture

Alongside this you will need to know how to lead your team into the action that effects real change. It needs both an understanding of the delicate creative process that allows ideas to emerge as well as a good understanding of how to shift behaviour and bring people on a journey.

REFLECTION: leading a workshop culture

- In the model shown in Figure 4.1, what areas do you personally need to pay most attention to – strategic thinking, design mindset, ideas to action or behaviour change?
- Which do you lean more towards – people or business? Thinking or doing?
- At this stage, what challenges do you foresee in introducing a workshop culture to your team?

Chapter 4 – key takeaways:

- Being successful in change means being clear on what you can and can't control or influence. Set out a clear plan and remember to celebrate progress.
- A workshop culture is a balance between people and business, thinking and doing, and understanding strategic thinking, design, turning ideas to action and behaviour change support this.

- Transforming your team's culture requires being ready to collaborate. This involves practising skills and abilities such as letting go of control, handling uncertainty, trust, openness and vulnerability.
- When you are preparing for guiding your team through and embedding a workshop culture, you are using very similar skills and approaches to running workshops.

We've now fully laid the foundations for understanding a workshop culture. We've taken a deep dive into the mindset, behaviour and skills that you need to lead your team towards this new way of working. Next, it's time to get more practical and look at what exactly you will do to involve your team.

PART 3

THE FRAMEWORK

The five-pillar framework for high-performing teams

In Part 3 we will cover a practical framework for implementation.

The next five chapters are extremely practical, and take you through a framework for building a workshop culture. They are packed with tips, exercises, templates and activities, so grab a notepad and pen, and let's get stuck in! Hold your vision for your workshop culture as we delve into the details of how to create one.

The framework is made up of five pillars:

1. **Alignment** – seeing the bigger picture
2. **Cohesion** – building self-awareness and empathy
3. **Communication** – meetings and workshops
4. **Design** – building new ways of working
5. **Change** – shifting behaviour and habits.

While this framework is set out in the order *Alignment, Cohesion, Communication, Design, Change,* you may find that there is a particular area that you want to address first based on the health of your team. (Visit www.workshopculture.co.uk for a brief assessment to identify where you might need to focus your time.)

Chapter 5

Alignment – seeing the bigger picture

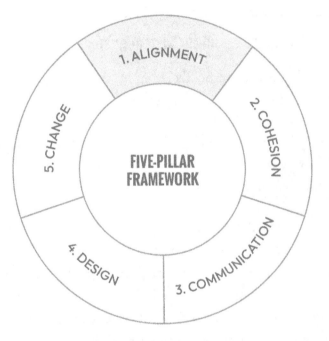

The first step in the practical implementation towards a workshop culture is to align your team around the bigger picture. This is about making sure you are all oriented in the same direction before you start any work. The earlier you identify and iron out any potential misalignment, the less chance it has of derailing your progress and potential later on.

In this chapter, we will look at how your team will also need to adopt a range of mindsets – growth, design, facilitation and change – so that you are all on the same page to start your transformation. We will also look at setting a compelling vision along with values and goals that point you all in the same direction.

By the end of this chapter, you will have learnt how to:

- think about the big picture as a team and understand how that increases motivation and engagement
- create values that connect your team and form your unique identity
- translate your team's ambitious goals into day-to-day behaviour.

CASE STUDY: speeding up through alignment

A lack of alignment can be like a tug of war. With people pulling in different directions, the team becomes rooted to the same spot.

I observed this with a wonderful team of highly talented individuals who were stuck because they were struggling to agree on the direction they wanted to take their venture.

When they formed as a team, they had very similar aspirations. As the years progressed, they gradually developed different goals for their own lives, which meant they each started to see the potential of the business differently. They hadn't realized how much they had each changed, and this was causing tension. As they had all been so close at the start of the business, they just couldn't understand how they weren't seeing eye-to-eye. Their relationship was breaking down, and the business wasn't moving forward as quickly as they hoped.

First I worked with each person individually to help them clarify and connect with their own core values. Then I worked with the whole group to assess whether there was alignment across their values and if they could continue to work together. It turned out that some of their individual values were so different that it was impossible to find a resolution, and they decided to part ways.

However, going through the process allowed each individual to connect much more strongly to what they wanted, and their own personal journey accelerated. Those who had similar strategic ideas stayed to grow the business, which is now thriving. Others pursued their own creative interests and found a new sense of happiness and purpose in their new career direction.

Although it was unfortunate that the team was no longer working together, lack of alignment was causing high levels of stress and burnout. By identifying this, we fast-tracked the inevitable so that no one wasted any more time working at cross purposes.

It is, of course, possible that when you start to build a workshop culture, a similar misalignment will be uncovered in your team. No amount of effort can resolve a fundamental difference in values. As a result, individuals may realize that they want to take a different direction in their work. While never easy, this eventually creates a better outcome for everyone involved.

Dynamic and fluid teams

The challenges we face shift on an almost daily basis. To stay resilient, our teams need the ability to adapt and respond as everything around us evolves.

We also need to change how we relate to the different teams we work in. According to research from the Center for Creative Leadership, most of us – 95% – are part of more than one team at a time.[1] If each team has its own dynamic and culture, it makes sense that we need to communicate differently across and within the different teams that we belong to.

This requires us to handle a certain amount of complexity and regularly context-switch. We're not able to change this fact, control the environment or slow things down, so a more effective outlook is to change our approach so that we can deal with whatever situation we find ourselves in at any given time.

Your unique team and context

We think a lot about how cultures can be different across different companies, but different subcultures can also exist across teams within one organization.

A range of factors contribute to your team's unique culture:

1. **The individuals on the team:** each person brings their own experience and skills, which means any one team will be as distinct as the mix of people of which it's made up.
2. **The work the team has to do:** the nature of the team's responsibilities influence the way they need to work – whether that's the speed, the timelines they work to, the people they interact with, or other specific requirements.
3. **The context:** how events, situations and other elements in the rest of the organization and wider external environment impact the team and their work.

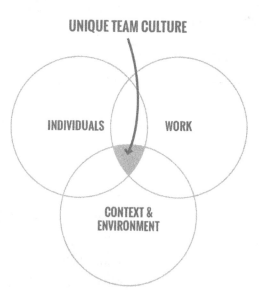

Figure 5.1 Your unique team culture.

As shown in Figure 5.1, the centre, where these factors overlap, forms your unique team culture. If something changes in any of these elements – for example someone joins or leaves the team, you start a new project, you transition to hybrid working, etc. – it will impact the culture of your team. That's why we need to be constantly monitoring, re-balancing and adapting accordingly.

You can also see these elements play out on a micro-level in a workshop. A facilitator can design one workshop, yet run it with different teams and reach a different outcome. The results depend on the individuals in the session and how they come together as a team. It can even be affected by external factors on the day and the mood the participants bring. A facilitator must always have an open mind and be prepared to switch their plans in response. We can learn from this approach when we're building a workshop culture.

The mindset of a dynamic team

As our teams become more fluid and flexible, as a leader, you will be responsible for setting the scene, and you can initiate the conversations to realign your team when there has been a change. Alongside this, everyone on your team needs to build the right attitude that will set you all up for success. We need to adopt an approach that keeps us learning and evolving together. This means being as concerned with having the relevant skills and mindset as we are with the details of our tasks.

There are four mindsets everyone on a team needs to develop when they are building a workshop culture:

1. a growth mindset
2. a design mindset
3. a facilitation mindset
4. a change mindset.

As shown in Figure 5.2, a growth mindset starts this process, as your team needs to adopt the core belief that it's possible to get better at collaboration. It gets your team into the right frame of mind and creates a strong *intention* for improving your culture. A design mindset and facilitation mindset give us the tools to *translate* our intention of better collaboration into more concrete ideas. Then finally, a change mindset helps us shift our behaviour and take *action*.

Figure 5.2 The mindset of a dynamic team.

Once this mindset shift has taken place, this approach has the potential to change your team's experience of work for the long term.

A design mindset, facilitation mindset and change mindset are all naturally embedded into the workshop culture five-pillar framework (and yes, you might also recognize them from the previous chapter).

Growth mindset is slightly different because it requires shifting some potentially long-held beliefs about how teams develop together, and so I'll explain a little more here.

The value of a growth mindset for building a successful team

In 2006, Carol Dweck, a Stanford psychologist, wrote the seminal book *Mindset.*[2] It allowed the education sector and beyond to understand more about how successful people excel at what they do. Having a growth mindset, which has now become a well-used phrase, means that you are committed to development through practice and persistence. With a growth mindset, personal improvement is not left to chance – you work at it. The opposite to a growth mindset is a fixed mindset, where you believe that talent can only be innate, it can't be improved.

If you have to work at it, then it says something negative about your ability.

We often have this romantic idea of a high-performing team. That once we get the right people (i.e. stars) together, everything will fall into place. We want to rely on the right chemistry and hope that people will just 'get it'. Sometimes we feel we shouldn't need to speak about how we collaborate, because if we're brilliant individually then we'll be brilliant together. We may even adopt a fixed mindset – if we need to speak about how we work together, then it's because we're struggling as a team.

Sometimes a team can just have that magic sauce. But more often than not, just like any successful relationship, it takes effort. This concept hasn't taken a strong enough hold in the workplace. We focus more on skill, talent and delivery than we do on building our connection as a team.

The reality is, just like our technical ability, collaboration is something we can get better at both as individuals and as a team. These more people-oriented skills – like emotional intelligence, listening, curiosity and patience – are the real heroes of high-performing teams, and we need to pay more attention to these intangible elements if we really want to succeed.

TRY THIS: cultivating a growth mindset in your team

From her research, Dweck demonstrated that once people learn the difference between a fixed and growth mindset they will start adopting the latter. In my experience, the awareness of this does shift the way a team thinks about their work.

What else can you do to cultivate a growth mindset in your team?

- Identify some specific challenges you've overcome together and discuss the positive growth you've experienced as a result.

- Explore how you've changed as a team over a time period, say the past six months. Reflect on the new behaviours you've cultivated over the time that you have worked together.
- When your team has displayed brilliant collaborative behaviour which has led to success, work together to break down exactly what you did to make the success happen, rather than just focusing on the result you achieved.

The bigger picture – setting your team's direction: alignment, clarity and purpose

If an aligned team is the launch pad for high performance, collective clarity is like rocket fuel. A facilitated workshop often helps teams to find shared meaning and get on the same page around their overall team purpose. Those micro-moments of clarity within an uncertain world are what bring a team together. It grounds them in mutual understanding, helps them to get to the heart of their challenges, and enables them to move forward. When a team is clear on what matters and the end goal, the specifics for getting there become less important. The team has more control over this themselves, and it reduces the temptation for micromanagement from their leader.

There is so much value in discussing your aspirations as a team. Your team has the opportunity to create the vision of not only what they want to achieve, but also of how they will collaborate to get there. Imagine the shift that comes from your team understanding that they get to choose who they are at work, shedding old expectations and creating their future together. So energizing!

A workshop setting is often the perfect environment for this kind of thinking, where we are encouraged to think 'outside the box'. Start your team off by exploring *possibilities* (what could we do together? What is our potential?) rather than deciding exactly what they're going to do – that can come later.

Team purpose for motivation

Having a clear sense of purpose and meaning plays a key part of being engaged at work. In *Drive: The Surprising Truth About What Motivates Us*, Daniel Pink notes that one of the three factors for motivating knowledge workers is that they are able to see how their contribution fits into a higher purpose (the other two factors are autonomy and mastery).[3] That bigger picture can only be seen if we take a step back and look broadly at the direction we are going in, and we need to do this collectively as a team.

Teams build connection when they explore their purpose together. They can see they are striving for the same results. And paradoxically, if they spend more time doing this, it provides more context and meaning to their day-to-day work. When a team firmly believes in their vision, it's so compelling that it becomes bigger than any problems they may encounter to get there. Creating this in the minds of your team will generate the motivation to build a workshop culture where they can become more accountable and empowered.

Team alignment as empowerment – the big picture

Our workplaces generally favour speed and execution, so taking this time to build alignment upfront can create a level of dissonance. We assign more value to checking off a large volume of tasks rather than going deeper into a few that will have a longer-term impact. As I covered in Chapter 4, illustrated by the Eisenhower Matrix, we all have those big important tasks that we never get around to because we're too busy fighting fires. Unfortunately, this means that we're not giving valuable time to something that could not only make a difference in our work, success and performance, but also in our own sense of enjoyment and engagement.

Big-picture thinking gives you and your team an opportunity to challenge yourselves. You step away from known and comfortable detail into seeing wider patterns that can give you new insights about your work. It is an outward-looking exercise that requires pulling yourselves out of the present. Where are themes emerging across your work? What else might you be able to do together?

A team builds up an amazing amount of collective knowledge through the work that they do. But this knowledge isn't always surfaced and harnessed effectively. Observations might be mentioned in passing at a regular meeting, but they're not given the time for deeper exploration to interrogate what it could mean for the future. Think about how empowered your team could be when they realize they are able to shape their work based on their own wisdom and experience.

What workshops can teach us about big-picture thinking

Part of what makes a workshop so effective is that the team are clear on what they want to achieve. They might not know the specific activities and the details of the discussion, but they know where they want to get to by the end of the workshop – in other words, their vision for the session. This clarity is what creates the forward energy to keep them on track and aligned. When they go off course, the facilitator is there to remind them of what they set out to do. When things get messy and confusing – as they often do in workshops – they will remember why they're there and their collective end goal.

At the start of a workshop, a facilitator may ask a group to set ground rules – how they will engage with each other throughout the session. Ground rules might relate to behaviours like not interrupting each other, building upon each other's ideas or being an active participant. It helps a team to act in a way that will be conducive to the environment and what they need to get done. What are you trying to achieve, and how do you need to act as a team to get there?

This is something we can apply directly to thinking about the broader big picture for a team: not only our vision, but also aligning on values and how a team wants to *be* together – our ground rules or team manifesto. 'High performance' means different things to different teams, and your values are what will help you define it for your unique culture.

Your team vision and values are two aspects that can keep you grounded as a team, especially when everything around you is unpredictable. Vision and values are what will keep a team going in the same direction. When we identify the purpose and desired outcomes of a workshop, then we can design a process and agenda that will keep us focused. In the same way, identifying your vision and values is like your team's compass for doing great work.

TRY THIS: how to run a big-picture thinking session

The first time you run a big-picture thinking session your team will need to be guided on what is expected of them. Inform them early on that their input is encouraged, and set expectations that this is an exploratory session to generate ideas – not everything will necessarily be taken forward.

A great big-picture thinking session will have three main areas:

1. reflecting on the past
2. bringing in outside influences for inspiration
3. looking forward to what's possible.

Reflecting on the past

Ask your team to honestly review their performance against any previous goals. This is not about blaming or shaming. It's merely to gather data about what you've learnt. It could be goals that were easy to achieve, goals that were difficult and why, what you've learnt about customers, clients or stakeholders or about the products or services you deliver. It's like an audit of performance.

Bringing in outside influences for inspiration

To ensure you're not operating in a complete bubble, take some time to review what's happening outside of your team, and if relevant, outside of your company or sector. What influences do your team feel might impact their work? What's interesting to them? What are they curious about?

Looking forward to what's possible

Now, using the content and data you've generated from reviewing your past performance and outside influences, what ideas does your team have for what you could do and how you could improve? What's on their wish list for things they would do if time and money weren't an issue?

The nature of these discussions will provide your team with enough content and stimulus to start shaping what you will do together and then set new goals.

Strategy development – ideas into action

You may find that your team becomes more invested in and connected to the success of a strategy when they are involved in creating it. The development of a clear strategy supports better and faster decision-making while getting the actual work done. After thinking about the broad direction of your team, you will need to select and prioritize the ideas that you will move forward with. This will set your path for a defined period (e.g. six months, a year) and will give the direction for what you do on a day-to-day basis.

A light warning: don't let your visioning sessions remain a conceptual exercise. This thinking is highly valuable, but it needs to lead to practical action within a reasonable timescale. If it doesn't, frustration and workshop fatigue can set in (more about workshop fatigue in Chapter 7). Remember that workshops are the start of the discussion and can create momentum, and then more work comes afterwards when the outputs are integrated into the business. Your team will need to commit to action and be accountable for seeing it through.

If you have generated new ideas that require further research, a new way of thinking or more resources, be aware that this will create a parallel track of work to your day-to-day. Team visioning sessions will generate additional, albeit valuable, work. You will be working both on the present (your existing tasks) and towards the future (the ideas that came out of your big-picture-thinking workshop) at the same time. This will be the case until your future vision becomes your current work and is incorporated into your regular tasks. That's evidence that you have stepped up into a new level as a team!

Back to reality

Start to match your ambitious goals with resources that you have access to (time, skills, budget, capacity), or make plans to acquire those resources. This is how you begin to bring your team strategy to life. Part of your role is in motivating your team, and at this point it will be a fine line between inspiring and overstretching them. Make sure that you are encouraging them just past what is comfortable but not so much that any tasks seem unachievable. As mentioned earlier, in *Drive*, Daniel Pink lists 'mastery' as one of three factors for employee motivation.[4] This means ensuring that people are working towards a level that is just above their existing ability to challenge them, but not too much that they become disheartened and frustrated.

This planning exercise also gives you the opportunity to be honest as a team about your strengths and weaknesses in relation to delivering the strategy you have developed. Have a real, open conversation about where you think you could struggle, team concerns and the challenges you might face. Assess your current situation and if necessary create a plan for bringing in or developing the new skills you will need in order to grow your capabilities. These open conversations are at the heart of a workshop culture and contribute to you continuously developing and improving as a team.

Setting collective team goals

Setting team goals – outcomes that you can only achieve together and that energize your team – will drive collective motivation and connection. It will help you to build and affirm your shared identity.

Find a way to keep your team accountable that works for everyone, and create a timeline to keep you on track. This will enable you to keep checking in and reviewing your progress in a supportive yet direct way. You may also like to define the different cycles that you work to so that you can build a cadence for keeping yourselves accountable. When does it make sense to assess whether the actions you are taking are having an impact? This can be at different levels: yearly, quarterly, monthly, weekly and daily. The ways of working that you design will match this (we cover this more in Chapter 8). Whatever system you use needs to ensure your actions are measurable, realistic and can be reviewed regularly.

Also encourage team members to set their own individual goals in line with the broader vision. Ask them to consider what they think is possible alongside their other commitments, and ensure that they do not conflict with team goals. A conversation around goal setting enables you to productively challenge each other. Are you all being too conservative or too ambitious? When you have created the open, collaborative environment that a workshop culture brings, your team will have the language to do this constructively. You will be able to cultivate mutual growth and development.

Crystallizing team values

A new ambitious vision for your team

When you've identified your wider vision and strategy and started to outline your goals, your team will also need a way of embodying this new identity. If you have created some new goals to achieve, it is likely that you might need to shift some ways of working to reach them.

New goals that you haven't attempted before are going to stretch your team. This is the nature of innovation. If you want to grow, everyone will need to regularly step outside what is natural and comfortable to reach new heights. It makes sense that there will be elements that you want to improve on. Identifying what they are and having conversations about how you will make those improvements is how you design new ways of working.

This is a good opportunity to review and, if necessary, reset your team values by connecting them to your vision. Do your current values align with your new goals? What kind of team do you need to be to reach your goals? What does the kind of team that achieves those goals look like? It might be that you want to be more curious, more accountable, more supportive, more patient or something else. Start identifying the desired behaviours and mindsets followed by the consistent actions your team needs to take to fit this identity.

Your values may evolve as your team develops. For example, if you want to encourage more experimentation as a team now, you might create a value that reflects this. Then when experimentation becomes more natural and embedded, you can shift your focus towards a new behaviour that you want to encourage.

Designing good values

Good values act like a GPS for your team. They are a constant guide and reminder of what you are striving to be. Good values help your team form a strong identity and communicate it to others. They can also act as filters for decision-making based on what you and your team have agreed is important. This creates more autonomy, as some decisions can be assessed against values rather than having to consult with others every time.

If your team has not articulated their values, the first step is to ask them what they think they are. Ask your team to recall projects, initiatives or achievements which represent your team's way of doing things. To gather additional data, you could go externally to other teams, and clients or customers if appropriate, and ask them what values they think your team embodies. Other people sometimes see qualities that you are not able to, and having this external view can help you identify how you want to be seen. At the very least, brainstorm what you *think* people might say about you, or go a step further to what you *want* people to be saying about you. Ultimately though, your values will come from the heart of your team. They have to feel and believe them to live them.

When you are refining your values, ensure they are unambiguous. Choose words that have the same meaning to everyone, and clarify any sentences or phrases with a follow-up description. Finally, bring your values to life with stories. Make them real by sharing examples of when team members have displayed these principles. This acts as inspiration for others to replicate and create their own examples.

Translating values into behaviour

The values that we create and repeat consistently through actions become who we are. Defining them is only the first step. For values to have true meaning they need to exist in the daily behaviour of your team. Get granular about what your team values look like when acted out – for example, 'we are curious' could mean we ask at least three questions before providing a solution.

Once you have finalized your values and behaviours, find a way of capturing them so they stay top of mind. Some teams like to visually represent their values using illustrations or create a slide deck to refer back to. You can combine this by regularly discussing them in your team meetings to keep your values alive. For example, ask each team member to share recent examples of when they've demonstrated the values or seen them in action. A step further is to weave your values into a reward system, either through informal celebration such as team recognition or an award, or more formally into employee performance reviews.

Being committed to living your values is one way to connect your bigger picture vision to your day-to-day and begin your transformation as a team.

Chapter 5 – key takeaways:

- Your team is unique, and there is no 'one size fits all' for better collaboration.
- Everything starts with a growth mindset. Your team needs to see collaboration as a skill that they can improve.
- Alignment is the starting point for a workshop culture. It grounds your team and sets the foundation for high performance.
- To translate team values into behaviours, get granular and specific about what they look like in action.

This chapter was all about orientating your team in the same direction with a clear vision and a collective team identity. In the next chapter we'll look at how to go deeper so that you can create the strong connection that builds empathy and trust.

Chapter 6

Cohesion –
self-awareness and connection

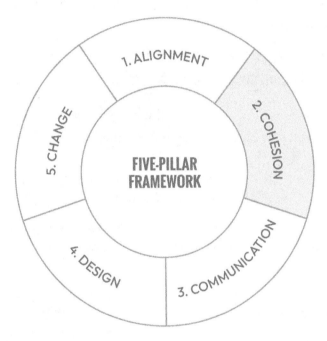

Now that you have aligned on your vision and values, each person needs to understand the part they play and their contribution to the team. This self-awareness and the resulting discussions will then create empathy across the team. This is a vital part of forming the strong connections that make work flow more easily. When cohesion is strong in a team, you can approach the more challenging areas of working together more effectively – giving and receiving feedback and dealing with conflict.

In Chapter 6 we look at the relationship between individual identity and team identity, and how building self-awareness will help your team to perform at its best.

By the end of this chapter, you will have learnt:

- a range of tools and techniques to help your team build self-awareness
- the conversations that encourage empathy and mutual growth in your team.

CASE STUDY: solving a personality clash

Even when a team is aligned on the bigger picture, a personality clash can still be a barrier to productive collaboration.

A team I worked with were very clear on their goals. They were delivering high-quality programmes and events that impacted a wide range of stakeholders. This team was highly aligned on what they needed to do, and on what 'good' looked like. Yet opinions on different approaches for how to run their programmes was causing resentment and frustration. It was preventing the team from making the best use of their resources.

In particular, two people had overlapping roles. They were almost at opposite ends of the spectrum in terms of their working styles. One person was high energy, straight-talking and laser-focused on results. They loved working long hours and would hammer out tasks in a way that seemed superhuman. The other team member focused more on relationship building. They had deep professional experience in dealing with their exact type of client and had new ideas for how to evolve their services. This person was passionate about their role but also wanted to take a more balanced approach to their working week.

Neither colleague could understand the other's approach, and they would each be frustrated when a decision was made that they didn't agree with. They would often clash in meetings or over long email chains. This was causing an uncomfortable and awkward environment for other people on the team. No one knew who to take instruction from, and team members would find themselves stuck in a power play. Time and energy were being spent on managing disagreements rather than having positive and exciting discussions about how they could deliver more value to their clients. What else could be possible if they weren't held up by these conflicts?

In this situation, we were able to quickly move through the Alignment pillar, and spent a lot of time encouraging deep conversations across the team so that everyone could understand more about each other's working styles.

I encouraged the team to create 'user manuals', reflecting on the following questions:

- What kind of work do I thrive on and in what environments?
- How can you get the best out of me?
- When do you not get the best out of me?
- What else would I like the team to know about me?

By using these questions as conversation starters, these two individuals started to see what impact their lack of cohesion was having on the rest of the team. They agreed to check in with themselves and each other before they reacted. They committed to being more curious and patient when the other did something they didn't understand, rather than jumping to judgement. They started to have conversations about how they could work together and use each other's strengths instead of constantly trying to force the other to work in a way that wasn't natural to them.

Balancing the team and individual

For a team to perform highly, the individuals in the team need to be able to do their best work. If planned well, a workshop will have the right people in the room so that there is a good representation of diverse expertise. From there, the facilitator will aim for a balance between bringing out individual contributions and combining those ideas into a collective whole. Well-facilitated workshops are an excellent format for serving individuals and groups at the same time. This is the same in a workshop culture. The ultimate goal is collaboration, but you can't get there without surfacing and celebrating the talent of the individuals.

Linda Hill describes this challenge in *Collective Genius*: 'Thus, leaders encourage and support the individuals in their groups because they are the source of ideas that constitute the raw material of innovation. Yet the ultimate innovation will almost always be a collective outcome, something devised through group interaction.'[1]

Great collaboration is not about everyone working together in the same way. It's about celebrating the variety of working styles on the team, and being comfortable with the tensions that might bring. Ultimately, it's in those tensions that the magic happens.

So, if the Alignment pillar is zooming out to look at the big picture, the Cohesion pillar is zooming in and focusing on the detail of how your team is made up and what everyone brings. Being able to look simultaneously from these two different vantage points supports high performance. Research from the Center for Advanced Human Resource Studies explored the relevance of role identification to a team's success. They found 'as team members gain awareness of the team's purpose and their individual roles and responsibilities, they achieve higher performance and are better equipped to respond to evolving demands.'[2] The more self-aware the individuals on a team, the more highly the team will perform. Tasha Eurich, an expert on self-awareness and author of *Insight: How to Succeed by Seeing Yourself*

Clearly, describes self-awareness as the 'meta-skill of the twenty-first century' stating that it leads to qualities such as 'emotional intelligence, empathy, influence, persuasion and collaboration'.[3] These are all elements that are central to a workshop culture.

Each member of your team needs to be self-aware and productive at an individual level for the team to thrive. At the team level, you'll need to negotiate across all of your different working styles to support the needs of the team as well as ensuring there is space for people to be themselves. After all, it's the people that make the team unique in the first place.

Building self-awareness for team performance

Personality tests are a starting point

Assessments and personality tests provide a relatively quick way to get an insight into how you operate. They are also big business – to the tune of $2 billion at the time of writing.[4] How many of us haven't been seduced by Myers-Briggs, Belbin, Enneagram, DISC, Strengthsfinder, Insights or one of the many other options on the market? Getting the results of a personality test is like having someone look inside your soul and tell you the things that you instinctively knew but didn't have a way of articulating. There is something very enticing about responding to a few questions and then having that result in a full profile of your character.

Personality tests are great as a simple entry point into self-awareness. For someone not used to regular reflection, it's an easy, non-threatening way of understanding how you might be seen by others. Secondly, it helps you to appreciate why you might regularly disagree with certain colleagues because of how you approach work differently. But they also have their limitations (as well as questions about their legitimacy[5]), and so we need to look at them as the first step in a longer process. After taking a personality test, it's important to analyse the results, discuss with your team, identify any points of conflict and then explore how you're going to move forward.

Alongside any assessments like this, your team should work to build an ongoing habit of reflection. Tap into certain reactions that you've had to an event or something that frustrated you, explore situations that keep repeating themselves; understand the tasks that you tend to flow through easily, how you deal with stress and challenges, your communication style, how you respond to different types of communication and your preferences in getting work done. Then use this real-life insight to support the data that you get from your personality tests.

The reflection habit

To become self-aware, we need to spend time in reflection. If you've ever worked for yourself, you know how important it is to be conscious of your own productivity and effectiveness. You are reliant on it to make a living. Yet reflection is not a widely accepted activity for employees during work time, despite there being evidence that it improves our performance.[6]

If we create space for reflection in our work, it will have a positive impact on our team. When we become more aware of what we personally need to do great work and what fulfils us, we can start to create those conditions for ourselves. Once we have recognized the value of our own contribution and connected that to the wider team purpose, we can readily step into our roles with meaning. If our workplaces give us permission to spend this time on reflection, it becomes a feature of our work. Great teams have this as a central conversation from which they build their success.

Three areas that each team member can build more self-awareness around are:

1. **Their unique skills and expertise** – what they bring to the team, as well as their opportunities for development.
2. **How they work** – when they are most productive and creative, tasks they enjoy or tasks they find difficult, etc.
3. **Collaboration skills** – their ability to work with others, and how they communicate and interact with people who have different ways of working.

REFLECTION: time to reflect

Review how much reflection currently takes place in your team:

- Does your team have the opportunity to reflect?
- How might you introduce more 'approved' reflection time? For example, can you give yourself and your team ten minutes each week?
- How might you improve the quality of individual reflection to ensure it is supporting team performance?

Self-awareness supports mutual growth in a team

When each person on a team is committed to building self-awareness, they can become clearer on what they are contributing and look honestly at the gaps in their performance that they might need to fill. This helps everyone understand what they might need to reinforce or develop to ensure that the entire team is able to move forward and make progress.

In particular, each person needs to be clear on their individual opportunity areas. And sharing this openly, within a psychologically safe environment, creates the foundation for mutual growth. Having these honest conversations requires vulnerability, but also helps to build accountability.

Team members can make commitments to changing their habits and ask others to check in on their progress. They can connect with colleagues that they want to learn from. They can encourage others when they are struggling, celebrate their efforts and help them see where they've moved forward, even when they may not see it themselves. They can affirm each other's qualities so that each person can also acknowledge their own skills, deepen them and grow more.

When this happens, you become more than colleagues – you become peer coaches and mentors to each other. There is no need for competition, because you have all identified your unique abilities and strengths. As you support each other, you each grow individually, and it benefits your overall team performance. That's true collaboration.

Individual productivity, team productivity

Collaboration doesn't mean a team has to constantly work side by side and always be available to respond to messages. That would be exhausting. People need time to process their thoughts and work individually. This is true even in workshops.

In fact, a 2018 study demonstrated that the most effective collaboration happens in 'bursts'. The research highlighted how high-performing teams collaborate 'intermittently', and those punctuated moments of collaboration (i.e. meetings, workshops and discussions) were supported by periods of individual working time.[7] This makes sense in the knowledge economy, as our currency is our thinking. We need to give ourselves and our colleagues the space and time to do what we do best. What happens in those 'in-between' times is vital to the success of the team. While online collaboration tools have made it much easier for us to stay in touch and communicate, we also need to find the balance or risk 'collaborative overload', where our time spent interacting with others is at the expense of our individual productivity.[8] Teams need to ensure that these tools and other collaboration methods do not get in the way of the time we need to allocate for important deep, focused work, defined by Cal Newport in *Deep Work* as 'professional activities performed in a state of distraction-free concentration that push your cognitive capabilities to their limit. These efforts create new value, improve your skill, and are hard to replicate.'[9]

This means that we need to explore our own ways of getting work done. Imposing a single way of working on everyone becomes counterproductive. A routine that optimizes someone's productivity and performance might be based on deeply personal factors such as their body clock (at the most basic level, whether they function better early in the day or later at night), their personal situation and where they are working from.

A workshop culture encourages this individual reflection and creates the space for us to share our own routines, current situations and anything that might be impacting or supporting our work. When we consider everyone's individual working styles, it makes a difference to the overall effectiveness of the team. With more teams working virtually and globally across multiple time zones, it becomes even more important to have conversations like these. Ultimately, individual productivity affects team productivity, so starting from here will breed better results.

Developing your productivity systems

Encourage each member of your team to build a personal productivity system that enhances their strengths and supports their weaknesses. The first step is for them to identify what they currently do to get their work done – for example, how they capture their tasks and plan their days and weeks. They will then work out their own routines that enable them to deliver their work to a high standard.

It takes ongoing experimentation and iteration to fully understand what is right for us. As our work and situations change, we learn more about what is effective and how we can optimize for productivity, engagement and performance. We might play around with our ideal morning routine or figure out the best times of the day or week for certain tasks (such as intense thinking or lower-level cognitive activity). We'll start to learn when we need to take breaks, go for a walk and take a step back. We might play around with how we capture our tasks or build our personal suite of digital apps.

This is not just for the productivity geeks. We all need to understand the habits we need to build and break to be great collaborators and communicators. Think of how athletes have their own personal workout and meal plan based on their unique body composition, muscle mass and metabolism. What works for one athlete will be different for another. The same is true for personal productivity.

Positive impact on the organization – shift in power and responsibility

This attention to our individual productivity and engagement will have a tremendous impact on our teams and the overall organization. When we have the time and space to explore our best ways of working, the business benefits in the long run.

A workshop culture is about treating employees as the adults they are, and trusting that they are best-placed to know how to deliver the work that they have been employed to do. This increased level of trust creates a shift in power and responsibility towards the employee. Some employees may not be used to this, especially those who have experience of working in organizations that have been more traditionally run, valuing power at the 'top'. Some may find it difficult to get used to this level of responsibility. Making the space for building self-awareness is an essential part of the process.

In a workshop culture, everyone's work and development is out there for all to see, and this supports the progress of the team (we look at the importance of transparency in Chapter 8). This transparency breeds trust and autonomy by supporting communication and surfacing any conflicts before they become a problem. With more empowered team members, the culture is both intentionally developed and becomes self-evolving. This openness creates a culture of continuous improvement, providing more potential for innovation and high performance.

Techniques for reflection and feedback

If your team is new to reflecting on their working style and productivity, here are some techniques to get started:

Mood tracking and journaling

In their research study for *The Progress Principle*, mentioned in Chapter 1, Amabile and Kramer asked people to complete a diary at the end of each day to track their mood.[10] If your team is developing a new reflection habit, simply starting to pay attention to how they feel at the end of a day could be extremely insightful in helping them to understand their working patterns. Ask questions like:

- On a scale of 1 to 10, how energized are you?
- What happened during the day, or what did you do that contributed towards this score?
- Can you identify any tasks or events that fuelled you, or any situations where you weren't using your full abilities?

You can also encourage your team to take this one step further into journaling – taking a set amount of time to write around a topic to process their thoughts. In *Exploratory Writing: Everyday Magic for Life and Work*, Alison Jones provides a number of creative techniques, writing conventions and brainstorming tools that help gather insights about our own thoughts. One of these techniques is freewriting – grabbing a blank sheet of paper and a pen, starting a timer and writing non-stop for six minutes.[11] The aim is not to censor ourselves, but to simply observe what emerges without judgement.

Team user manual

The next step on from the kind of freewriting used in journaling is to use writing prompts. If you'd like to provide yourself and your team with a more structured way to reflect, consider crafting some work-related questions.

The 'user manual' technique has become popular for teams to build connection since being shared by former CEO Ivar Kroghrud in a 2013 *New York Times* article.[12] Each person responds to a list of questions about how they work and communicate.

I shared some examples in the case study at the start of this chapter. Some other questions could be:

- What times of day am I most productive?
- How do I get my best ideas?
- What is my ideal working set-up?
- What kind of work do I find challenging?
- How do I like to receive feedback?

Teammates then share this with each other to understand a bit more about what makes their teammates tick (or what they get ticked off about!).

Asking others

If your team is open to honest and constructive feedback, each person can gather opinions from others to understand how they are viewed in the team. Some tools, such as 360 degree assessments, already build this in, but you can choose to do it more informally. If you do, encourage your team to be specific about the kind of feedback they are seeking – for example, the skills and traits they are looking to improve, where they are already displaying them and where they have opportunities to do it more. This also helps the person providing the feedback to know what to focus on. You could set this up as a team meeting and use breakout groups of two or three people to give and receive feedback. Each person on your team can create their own personal dashboard for self-improvement that they can start to make real progress on.

TRY THIS: team user manual

- Gather a list of questions from your team that they would like others to answer and would like to answer themselves.
- Use these questions to create a template for your team user manual.
- In a workshop setting, ask everyone to complete the user manual and share their responses.
- From everyone's responses, create a shareable and editable resource that the team can continue to refer to.

Building empathy for team cohesion

Once your team has built more self-awareness and started to understand their own patterns on an individual basis, the next step is to encourage them to articulate it at the team level. When people start to understand their own patterns, they become more understanding of themselves, become more understanding of others and become more understood! There is comfort in being appreciated for who you are, and a sense of relief and freedom that you don't need to hide your quirky ways of working. Naturally there will be similarities across your team – maybe in outlooks, passions and personal values – and you will also find differences. It's in the differences that there is the most opportunity, and this also creates the foundation for empathy.

Empathy is defined by *Merriam-Webster* as 'the action of understanding, being aware of, being sensitive to, and vicariously experiencing the feelings, thoughts, and experience of another'.[13] Like many of the traits we've been exploring throughout this book, empathy is a skill that can be developed and a real superpower that not only creates new insights, but improves relationships. Building empathy requires asking more questions before jumping to judgements or conclusions about why people act in a certain way. It involves patience and having a true sense of care towards others. Empathy enables people to feel seen, heard and appreciated. This has a wonderful impact on teams. Empathetic environments are compassionate and inclusive. They bring out the best in people, and unproductive conflict often melts away.

The 'empathy map canvas', a tool created by Dave Gray (shown in Figure 6.1), helps teams understand what their customers might feel, think, say or do so that they can build better products and services.[14] It's also a great tool to use within and across teams.

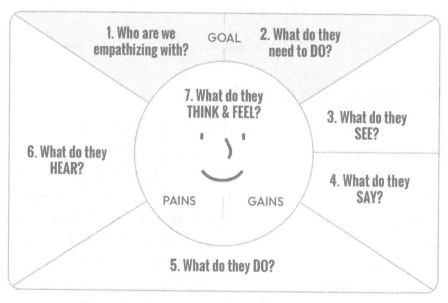

Figure 6.1 The empathy map canvas by Dave Gray.
Reproduced with permission.

Through deep curiosity, we can use the empathy map canvas to step into our colleagues' shoes to explore what they might be seeing and experiencing. Then with those insights, we can create new ways of relating to each other.

TRY THIS: empathy map canvas

Does your team experience ongoing conflict with another department in your organization? Use the empathy map canvas to sketch out a profile for the people in that department. What new insights does your team gather from completing the empathy map canvas? How might you change your approach for interacting with the other department to improve the relationship?

Empathy for resolving conflict and celebrating diversity

When there are tensions getting in the way of a team making progress, practising empathy can help to resolve this conflict. If there is a clash of personality or working styles, a breakdown of communication or a misunderstanding will negatively impact how people relate to each other and get their work done. If not addressed, it starts to grow, bubble away under the surface and become more ingrained into the culture. When we find ourselves caught in this cycle of unproductive conflict, we can go back to empathy and self-awareness to understand why the people involved are acting or responding in the way that they are.

When empathy is embedded into our team culture, it makes this type of conflict less likely to occur in the first place. The more empathy we create, the more we increase our capacity for understanding others' differences. Bring the multitude of working styles within your team to the surface, and normalize each and every one of the differences. People can learn from each other and teach new ways of doing things, and this will contribute to the team creating their own unique methods of working.

A great team is about celebrating all of the diversity within the team, including the way that we work, and having the resilience and the aptitude to work with differences even if it makes us uncomfortable. When we build empathy in a team, we create the conditions for appreciating more diversity and inclusion.

Chapter 6 – key takeaways:

- Even if a team is aligned on their vision, personality clashes will be a barrier to high performance.
- Self-awareness can start with personality tests, but this needs to be supported with deeper discussions and regular reflection.
- If we want more flexibility and freedom in our teams, this must be supported by more open communication and transparency.
- Building self-awareness creates empathy so that we can manage conflict effectively if it arises.

The exercises and conversation starters I've shared in this chapter will help everyone on your team understand and relate to each other more effectively. This starts you on the road to better communication, particularly in your meetings, which is the focus of Chapter 7.

Chapter 7

Communication – meetings and workshops

The central pillar of the workshop culture framework is Communication. How we communicate and collaborate as a team is heavily influenced by our meetings and how we interact in them. Unsurprisingly, facilitation plays a very key part in setting this up.

Chapter 1 covered how bad meetings can hurt an organization. This chapter gives a practical guide for meetings which have a positive impact and contribute towards a workshop culture.

We cover how to encourage everyone on your team to facilitate, and provide tips for building these core skills.

By end of the chapter, you will have learnt how to:

- ensure that each meeting you run has a clear purpose and is designed to make the impact it needs
- bring more facilitation into your regular meetings by using some simple techniques
- build a meeting rhythm that connects your team and forms the central part of your team communication.

CASE STUDY: meeting rhythms for better communication

'We should run more of our meetings like workshops'. This was music to my ears at the end of a facilitation-skills training session I'd run. The team was taking the training to improve how they collaborated with their service users. By the end, they had seen the value of introducing workshop techniques to improve the way that they worked together themselves. This is one of the goals of a workshop culture – to have facilitation as a central approach to the way a team works.

This is exactly what I aimed to do with another senior team that I worked with. The company – a thriving creative agency – was growing quickly, and the CEO wanted to address how the culture was adapting to ensure that collaboration remained at the core. The nature of the company meant that different departments had to work together seamlessly to serve their clients. To make sure this was working well, we first had to make sure it was happening at a leadership level.

The senior team was relatively new in its makeup – some team members were stepping into more management-level roles, some headed up departments that operated independently. They hadn't come together in this way before or had the opportunity to form their identity as a senior team.

The meetings they did have were highly functional, and as their pipeline was full with client projects, didn't provide the space for the team to have conversations about what was happening across the business. They also didn't have time for more strategic conversations about where the company was going.

After working through the Alignment and Cohesion pillars, our programme focused on opening up communication between departments so that the members of the senior team could form stronger connections. The CEO intended to step away from the day-to-day running of the company and so wanted to empower the senior team to make decisions together. We looked closely at the type of meetings they needed to have and the frequency of those meetings – whether weekly, monthly, quarterly and annually. We also looked at what needed to happen in each of those meetings for them to stay fully aware of any urgent challenges as well as discussing higher-level issues such as processes, staff development and client management.

Impactful meetings use design and facilitation

Meetings are the linchpin of our modern organizations. Work in the knowledge economy relies not just on the tasks, but also the relationships between the tasks. Many of these relationships are developed in meetings. The way you meet and run your meetings has a big impact on culture. When people meet in a productive way (e.g. in well-facilitated workshops), magic happens, and in this book, we've been unpicking what that means so that we can apply it practically and holistically across our teams.

As I covered in Chapter 1, bad meetings are our number one reason for why a workshop culture is needed. (If this is the only thing you solve as a result of reading this book, I promise it will already make a difference!) Many meetings are nothing but unstructured discussions full of personal opinions, egos, and politics, and we have far too many of them. There may be a meeting agenda, but not much thought goes into how those conversations should happen based on desired outcomes. This means there's no differentiation between an update meeting, a meeting where a decision needs to be made or a meeting where a team needs to generate ideas together. In fact, each type of meeting has a different purpose and a different energy, and both elements should be considered to create the right structure.

If you think about approaching your meetings in the same way you would approach a workshop, it means they also need to be designed – both at a strategic level and a tactical level. Strategically, a team needs to look at all the different types of meetings they must have for the work they need to get done. When you look at this effectively, you will find that your meetings have a variety of purposes, lengths and formats. Then tactically we need to look at what happens in each of those meetings.

Facilitation skills for everyone

As we covered in Chapter 4, having a design mindset and facilitation skills is important for you as a leader when you are building a workshop culture within your team. Facilitation is a valuable leadership skill, but that doesn't mean it should only be reserved for official team leaders. Team members benefit from better facilitated meetings, and they benefit when they have the opportunity to facilitate too. When these principles are adopted across all members of a team, they become even more powerful. Both design and facilitation are applied quite literally through the process of building a workshop culture, as we'll soon explore. And, as we covered in Chapter 5 (the mindset of a dynamic team), it makes it much easier if everyone on the team understands these skills. These skills are not just for one or a few people. Design and facilitation need to become natural, inherent behaviours in a team.

Facilitation skills also create better communication and empathy across the team. It means that everyone can take the role of supporting better meetings and conversations. Understanding the approach can supercharge a team's effectiveness. By rotating the role of facilitator, every team member can experience what it's like to lead in a creative and collaborative environment.

With design and facilitation skills embedded across a team, everyone is able to play an active part in introducing a workshop culture. When everyone has these skills, it empowers anyone to identify and raise any problems. If your team falls off track, there will always be someone to keep you all accountable and remind you to come back to these principles. It then becomes everyone's responsibility to make teamwork better, which means more self-sustaining, high-performing teams and reduces the risk of micromanagement.

Not just better meetings – better communication

The impact of bringing more facilitation in your meetings starts to change the way everyone in your team relates to each other. When people are invited to speak up, this has two results – how people feel about their contribution to the team, and how people connect.

More people speaking up means more ideas are heard, and that brings more knowledge across the team about what people think as well as their talents and insights. Teammates get to know each other when there is productive and inclusive conversation, and this creates the space for better connection and relationships. When meetings are facilitated well, it connects the tasks and the people doing them by improving overall communication.

Better facilitated meetings train people to have better conversations, ask better questions and make it easier for them to approach their teammates. They know who to go to and who has what expertise, and they will feel more comfortable asking for help.

Work is more than just delivering tasks, and meetings set the foundation for how a team works together. They are the space where the team culture becomes highly visible and gets reinforced.

How to encourage more facilitation in your team

So how do you ensure that everyone on your team has these skills? One way is to demonstrate the value of the skills through the approaches we'll lay out in the next part of this chapter. By making well-facilitated meetings the norm rather than the exception, your team will come to expect it as the way things are done. When teams see that it gets results, they'll get curious and want to learn these skills themselves.

Another way is to rotate the role of facilitator around your team. Once they have observed facilitation in action, give people the opportunity to design and lead meetings regularly, presented as a learning opportunity rather than a need for polished results. This will create a practice ground for your team as well as ensuring your meetings stay fresh through the different facilitation styles.

A workshop culture also encourages teams to bring core facilitation skills into their ways of working so they will be also practising them outside the setting of a meeting. As we explored in Chapter 4, skills like asking better questions, active listening, dealing with chaos and synthesis can all be demonstrated in daily work.

TRY THIS: facilitation for everyone

Rotate the role of facilitator in your team so that everyone has an opportunity to practice running more effective meetings.

The responsibility of a meeting facilitator

As facilitators, it's our responsibility to make our workshops as effective as possible, taking ownership of the *process* from preparation through to running the workshop or meeting and finally supporting the follow-up. The participants take care of the *content*. When we are able to maintain the quality and impact of workshops, we maintain their potency. When people consistently experience bad workshops, they get tired of the format. This is exactly what has happened with meetings. Although they are a vital part of progress in organizations, the consistent mismanagement of them has caused people to grow weary.

We need knowledge of a range of areas that we can apply to our meetings to make them more effective:

- **Group dynamics** – awareness of the factors that support creative collaboration and the biases that groups display that can get in the way of a great discussion. How can we design a session that optimizes for creativity, productivity and inclusion?
- **Understanding the context** – clarity on the purpose of the session we are running, the desired outcomes, and the relationships and history that exists in the team. What has happened up to this point in time, and how might that affect what needs to happen in the meeting?
- **A commitment to progress** – a pragmatic approach towards the outcomes of the meeting and the team's ability to implement them. What might prevent them from taking action after the session, and what can we design into the meeting to support them in moving forward?

Crafting a meeting outline is a creative task and involves letting go of your preconceived ideas of what will happen during the session. You will start with a blank canvas and define the boundaries (i.e. the meeting agenda or outline), but it's the team that will fill it in. Traditional management tells us that the role of leaders is to monitor and direct everything that an employee is doing to get to the outcome they have already decided. A workshop (and workshop culture) flips this on its head. A workshop facilitator knows that they cannot control the outcome of a session. They just need to do everything they can to put the foundations in place for the team to get to the outcome in the way that is best for them. It's a balance between providing a framework but then stepping away for the team to complete the details. If we do this in our meetings too, we can achieve great results.

Providing autonomy and agency

Workshops empower participants to come up with their own ideas and answers to big questions. The facilitator crafts and poses questions to guide the team towards breakthroughs. This directly affects how engaged participants feel during the session, and also how they feel about the work they go on to do. The role of the facilitator is to encourage buy-in and ownership, not dictate.

Our meetings are often seen as mechanisms for transmitting information rather than involving people in the problem-solving process, when the latter is the most compelling motive for bringing people together. Information and facts can simply be shared asynchronously. The most valuable reason to bring people together is to ask questions, get their views and generate a discussion. They will feel consulted, part of the solution, and you gain more support.

This applies to *process* as much as it does to *content*. Teams that are supported to find their own ways of working together, rather than being told how to, are more likely to stick to those new behaviours. An impactful way to make change happen is for people to be part of the change themselves in a co-creative process. This provides more autonomy and agency, which supports more engagement and high performance at work.

Supporting open conversations

Co-creation is a team-building exercise in itself. As well as developing ideas for what you're going to work on together, you can address team dynamics, process, blockers, conflict, barriers and more all at the same time. It provides an opportunity for teams to reflect and look closely at what might be getting in their way of doing good work. The point at which a team is ready to have the difficult and honest conversations about what might be blocking them is the same point where growth and breakthroughs can happen.

These types of conversations are about the space in between the tasks that you have to do as a team. These are the conversations that make getting work done easier. They bring any obstacles to the centre and recognize them as an integral part of learning and growing together. They help teams to realize the freedom and ownership they can take over how they work, expose what's getting in their way, as well as encouraging them to collectively find solutions. The outcome may be a new way of working or a process or a habit to experiment with. This is about applying the principles of design thinking and creative problem-solving.

Making time to talk about these aspects is one of the keys to high performance, but it can be difficult. It's important to recognize that this *is* work – not a side aspect of it – and using facilitation techniques makes these conversations possible.

Avoiding workshop and meeting fatigue

When you are building a workshop culture, you are making a commitment to running impactful meetings. This means taking responsibility for how they are experienced by others. When you start to run more workshops, and more workshop-like meetings, they need to be run purposefully and effectively, and in their true spirit. If they are not, your colleagues may start to experience 'workshop fatigue'.

There has been a tendency in the working world to use the word 'workshop' lightly. It's even become a verb – 'workshopping'! The intention is to convey more collaboration and interaction or even just the generation of ideas. But sometimes what attendees experience is a badly-run meeting, except with some sticky notes and a white-board because they have come to be visible symbols of brainstorming sessions. In fact, these tools are just the surface, as we've seen so far by digging into the elements of what makes a true workshop.

The problem with doing this repeatedly is that people get tired of 'workshops' and lose faith in the format. This makes it harder to get buy-in for sessions when people have experienced so many ineffective ones in the past. People start to resist them as much as they resist going to their regular meetings. We lose the opportunity to show people what is possible through the power of workshops.

So the solution to this is to ensure that when you call a workshop, it really is that – you take the time to prepare and follow up, and avoid calling your more traditionally run meetings 'workshops' until they truly become more collaborative. Let your colleagues come to the conclusion that your meetings are more like workshops themselves.

Make your meetings more workshop-like

The most immediate thing you can do to improve your meetings is to make them more workshop-like. This is easiest to do when you're running sessions where you need to get work done and develop ideas – the focus is on the content you produce. These are sessions that develop projects, like strategy discussions, brainstorming, project kick-offs, and goal-setting workshops. They are very much about moving forward so a team feels a sense of progress.

With these more content-oriented sessions, collaboration is still important, although it's invisible and in the background. The participants are focusing heavily on the 'what', and the job of the facilitator is to focus on the 'how'. The participants are often not aware of the collaboration taking place, they are just immersed in a positive and productive experience. However, if you are in the facilitator role, you will be very aware that it's the team dynamics that either help or hinder progress. It's the politics and tension that might exist in a team that prevent them from moving forward, not the lack of ideas.

If you start making your meetings more workshop-like, and are able to make a great impact – including in the follow-up – you will gain buy-in to run more of them. We'll talk about another type of meeting / workshop later – the process-oriented 'workshop culture' session. These are much harder to convince people to participate in, first of all, because if there is already resistance to workshops, these sessions initially feel like a distraction from work. The irony is that they make work much easier.

Purpose, outputs and questions

To get into a facilitation mindset when you are planning your meetings, a good tool to help you prepare is the 'purpose-outputs-questions' template (Figure 7.1). It enables you to do two things:

1. set a clear intention for your meeting, and clarify what you are working towards
2. shift you into being curious and into thinking about how you are going to encourage participants to contribute content.

Before you start deciding on timings, activities and structure of your meeting, take at least 15 minutes to go through this exercise.

PURPOSE AND OUTCOMES:	OUTPUTS:
e.g. project check-in to review progress and plan next stages	e.g. reset timeline, a list of outstanding tasks

QUESTIONS:

e.g.
What has gone well so far?
What new information do we have?
What have we learned?
What needs to change?
What further questions or unknowns are there at this stage?

Figure 7.1 Purpose, outputs, questions template.

Purpose and outcomes: why are you holding this meeting? What is your ideal outcome? What is the overall goal? These will be more intangible results like: 'gain alignment', 'get clarity', 'build connection'. Consider how you want people to feel at the end of the meeting. What experience do you want them to have?

Outputs: what do you need to produce as a result of this meeting? What is the content that you hope to have by the end? This will be a list of more specific items, for example: a list of action points, a Q1 plan, a task list, some prototypes. Think specifically about what will be most useful to have once the meeting is finished and you're back into work. What will help you move a project forward?

Questions: as the facilitator, what do you want to know from the people attending the workshop or meeting? They will have knowledge that you do not (if they don't, then you should be participating rather than facilitating!) or opinions and ideas you are looking to uncover. How can you encourage them to share this knowledge? Step into the position of someone looking to learn, and think about what you're genuinely curious to find out. Brainstorm a list of questions without worrying if you repeat yourself. Keep going, and when you think you've finished, push yourself to come up with a few more.

Now look over your list of questions and group together those that have a similar theme or topic. These different themes or topics will likely be the areas of your meeting that you need to cover, and you've started to get an idea of the structure.

Doing this exercise helps you to ensure that you're covering what's important in your meeting. It also helps you see whether you're trying to achieve too much in one sitting, and whether you might need more than one meeting, or another format, to get through everything.

Designing meetings and workshops

When you have a clear idea of what needs to be covered in your meeting or workshop, you can then move into designing the structure. You will bring all of those elements from the purpose-outputs-questions exercise together into creating your session outline. This will be like a narrative that makes sense to your participants by the time they have got to the end.

You are using design to give you a direction and a foundation. There may be a need to change on the day, but with this planning you know you have done the best with the knowledge you have, and you will be more prepared if something unexpected happens. You can positively influence group dynamics by applying some design and preparation, and when you learn more about this, you can apply this to the wider area of teamwork too.

You're thinking about who will be in the room, what they need to discuss, and you're designing the appropriate sequence and guide for it. You will have thought about the challenge and identified the right problem(s) to solve. It's worth remembering that most facilitators can lead excellent workshops without any content knowledge or subject expertise because they're focused on the process.

You can find a wide range of types of meeting and workshop exercises in books, online and by learning from others, and a good facilitator will know how to run them step by step. A great facilitator, on the other hand, will take those exercises and make them their own, depending on the people who will be in the room and the context. Your exercises and activities are your toolkit; your design skills help you to apply them in the most appropriate context.

Applying strategic thinking to planning meetings and workshops

Strategic thinking is an essential part of designing and facilitating great meetings and workshops. To facilitate well, you need to value the entire process and picture the desired outcomes, while staying focused on what is happening in the room in the present moment. In the design stage of planning a meeting, if you start selecting activities (the detail) before understanding the purpose (the bigger picture), you might have a good workshop outline, but the content may end up disconnected and unfocused.

While designing a great workshop means thinking about the end goal and where you want to be by the end of the session, it is also about thinking beyond that. It includes thinking about where the results of a session will fit into a team's daily work. A great facilitator sees their role not just as creating a great experience on the day, but also as helping the participants bring the value back into their work and creating the bridge between idea and reality.

This requires thinking about the entire experience and how that impacts the people that are a part of it. You're looking at the end-to-end process, and exploring how to make the best of everyone involved. There will be some complexity to this, but your role as a facilitator is to try to make sense of it and turn it into something that can be practically applied. One way you can do this is by ensuring each participant commits to an action at the end of the session, and then finding ways for them to stay accountable.

Facilitation techniques to improve your meetings

First impressions count in great meetings. Start it in a way that signals to your team that they will be interacting and participating. Create an inviting and safe environment that gets people comfortable to speak up. Getting them to interact, even in a small way, as early on in the meeting as possible switches them on and encourages them to engage. This has been identified as the 'activation phenomenon' by Atul Gawande in *The Checklist Manifesto,*[1] where 'giving people a chance to say something at the start seemed to activate their sense of participation and responsibility and their willingness to speak up'. Observing this in medical teams, Gawande found that when people introduced themselves before surgery, this increased the chances of a team member pointing out a potential mistake later on. To adopt this method for your team, you could encourage people to speak up early by creating a short breakout discussion (even just two minutes) before you start the formal part of the meeting or workshop.

It may sound odd to say for a team environment, but the simplest way to engage someone is to get them to temporarily focus on themselves. This immediately gets their attention and shows that they can connect to the topic of the meeting. It's why reflection questions are so powerful. Check-ins – which are simple questions asked for every meeting attendee to respond to – at the start of meetings can impact a meeting's success in various ways. As well as the activation phenomenon, it creates a moment of mindfulness. Check-in questions might be something quick ('rate your mood on a scale of 1 to 10') or something more detailed ('what are you most looking forward to this week?'). Either way, they mark the start of a meeting. In our organizations, people are in back-to-back meetings, particularly if they are run virtually. A check-in enables them to pause, take a moment and switch their context. It also helps the facilitator and the participants alike to temperature check and feel the mood of the meeting.

Another way to ensure your meetings are inclusive, when it's appropriate, is to enable people to openly share their thoughts about what you'll be focusing on. People will already have their ideas, opinions and even baggage in relation to the topic that will be discussed, and giving them space to share this shapes the meeting around their existing views, meaning they will immediately be more invested. I like to call this kind of exercise a 'braindump', and if it works for your meeting, you can even shape the agenda around what emerges.

Managing the conversation

As well as ensuring an inclusive environment, the conversation needs to be fruitful and productive. In designing your session, you will have created the structure to move through various topics of discussion, but you will still need to ensure you stay on track and monitor any dynamics that might surface.

There may be people that are dominating the conversation, making long points that derail the direction, some that aren't contributing or others introducing unproductive conflict. Your role as facilitator is to acknowledge everyone's contribution, but bring them back to the focus.

Our definition of an effective meeting may be one that is efficient and moves through agenda points quickly. It is controlled by a chair who keeps the conversation succinct and brief. There is often a good case for this, but when we bring more creative thinking and workshop-style activities to our meetings, there may be moments when attendees feel slightly overwhelmed. It may feel messy, but that is a natural part of the process. It is your role as a facilitator to be so confident in your process that you know it will work out in the end, however it progresses. That's because you are clear on the purpose, you understand the context and you know the end point you are trying to reach.

When you need to bring the discussion back on track, thank people for their contribution and remind them of (1) the focus of the session and outcomes you need to achieve and (2) the time you have left in the session. Any interesting conversation points can be captured and returned to if there is time, or as part of another meeting.

Individual thinking and breakout groups

A workshop technique that can be powerful in meetings is when you provide attendees with discussion and reflection time away from the full group. Our traditional meetings are geared towards getting through as many agenda points as possible, and so we try to pack lots in. The disadvantage of this is that we only get superficial coverage of important topics. This unconsciously indicates that 'thinking' should take place outside of meetings to save time. But the truth is that, with our other demands, this rarely happens.

Instead, we should see meetings as valuable times to get talented people together to think deeply and problem-solve. This will, in turn, increase the quality of work done outside of the meeting. In our bias for efficiency, it may feel odd to allocate meeting time to individual thinking time and reflection, but this benefits a team in many ways. Firstly, the thinking gets done rather than dropping in priority and being squeezed last minute between other tasks. Secondly, we make space for introverted or neurodivergent team members to interact fully in a group setting, giving them to time to think about their responses before they are asked to contribute.

The next step on from individual thinking is breakout groups, where we split people off from the main discussion into pairs or smaller groups to process or digest a topic. Then they return to feedback to the whole group. This is possible both in-person and online with the right platform. Breakout groups enable a deeper discussion between fewer participants, and encourage those who feel self-conscious speaking up in front of a larger group to air their views in a more intimate setting. For teams doing this on a regular basis, it helps people build closer relationships.

Visual thinking

Although someone may take notes in meetings, what we see most is people speaking *at* each other. While this is not a problem in itself, it can become more powerful when we add a visual element to what is being said and heard. The discipline of graphic facilitation – the use of images to capture content in meetings and workshops – is a popular technique to help us record information visually. As shared earlier, these sketches can form useful 'artifacts' that help to us to make conversations more focused.

Figure 7.2 Graphic facilitation.

Image reproduced with permission from Scriberia.

Capturing content visually can mean sketches, and it can mean text-based information in bite-sized pieces, hence the popularity of sticky notes. We can arrange these bits of content to see where people are agreeing or points of tension, identify common themes and clarify our thoughts.

Recording the discussion visually also promotes inclusivity. When someone's idea or thought is added to a board – whether physical or digital – it shows that their point has been acknowledged. And when we enable people to contribute content simultaneously, for example by adding sticky notes to a board at the same time, it means that everyone's contributions can be recognized without them necessarily needing to speak it out loud.

A holistic look at our meetings

There are many different types of meetings and workshops we could run, but we rarely differentiate between them. We sometimes even try to cover many different types of meetings within one sitting. We know from our work that it's not easy to move quickly from admin to tasks that require deeper thinking, and research demonstrates that task-switching affects performance and productivity.[2] Yet we do this in our meetings time and time again.

Firstly, take a look at your team and what you want to achieve – your vision. What do you need to meet about and discuss as a team to reach the success levels you've set for yourselves? There might be client meetings, briefing meetings, idea generation, update meetings, forward planning, review meetings, feedback sessions, problem-solving, ad-hoc crisis meetings and more.

Then take each of those meetings separately, and briefly use the purpose-outcomes-questions template for each. Think about how the format differs across them – how long will they be, and what activities can you use to generate a great discussion?

A workshop culture is about challenging our existing notions of meetings and introducing new formats. This is about showing people different ways of working, which may be uncomfortable. So rather than changing everything at once, introduce them slowly and in tasters (remember foundation 3: small steps, not sweeping changes – see Chapter 3). You can bring a ten-minute workshop-style activity to a regular meeting to give people the experience. Not all meetings need to be a full workshop, but consider those where you do really need input from the team and where injecting more interaction would make it effective.

Find the right rhythm for your meetings

Once you've clarified clearly the different types of meetings you have across your team, identify which of those meetings would be useful to have regularly, which might be one-off meetings, and which ones might be held as and when the need arises. For meetings that need to be regular, identify the frequency you need to hold them at – daily, weekly, fortnightly, monthly, quarterly, or annually.

MEETING NAME	PURPOSE	OUTPUTS	FORMAT	FREQUENCY
e.g. Check in	To identify any blockers to progress and problem-solve	Solutions to problems, further conversations to have	1 hour, virtual	Weekly
e.g. Team planning session	To re-align around team goals and plan forward	Goals for next quarter	3 hours, in person	Quarterly

Figure 7.3 Meeting-rhythms template.

At this stage you have a *draft* meeting rhythm, which is a great way of keeping your team's momentum going and building accountability. You will have clear, separate and distinct purposes and formats of discussions that you can facilitate appropriately, improving the productivity of each of these sessions.

It's worth reiterating that this is a draft meeting rhythm. While you want to reduce cognitive load by planning all this out, when you get into the routine, you may find that some meetings aren't needed, you need to add another one in or a format has stopped working. You can review whether you need to switch the rhythm up again to stoke the energy of your team. This is all part of the ongoing conversation about how you work together and encouraging people to speak up if something needs improving.

'Workshop culture' sessions

When you're creating a workshop culture, you'll also introduce a completely new kind of regular meeting – the sessions you'll run to discuss how you work together. This is less about the actual work you'll get done and more about designing and experimenting with the process you use to do the work. Stick with me, this might get a bit meta!

These sessions are like all the elements of a workshop culture rolled into one. You'll be stepping away from your to-do lists to talk objectively about how you get it done. You'll be considering all of your individuals on the team and co-creating how you collaborate (I told you – meta!). You'll be in deep facilitation mode, asking questions and being curious, and you'll need to explore which habits and behaviours you need to modify.

I described earlier how these sessions are more difficult to get buy-in for, as they feel slightly removed from the actual work. However, they are essential to building a high-performing team. They work by cultivating reflection and intention into your team's ways of working. They encourage you to look at patterns, and assess what's contributing to your success and what might be getting in the way. They create owner-ship and accountability across a team, build transparency and reduce blame.

'Workshop culture' sessions need to be built into your meeting rhythms like your other meetings. Eventually they will become second nature to the work itself, and you will see the impact it has on the way you work together.

What happens after your meetings?

I covered in Chapter 1 how a workshop culture means that workshops are more than a one-off event and in Chapter 4 how the follow-up is essential. To ensure your meetings are fully impactful, you also need to consider the work that will happen afterwards – for both the attendees and you as the facilitator. How will the content, ideas and discussion be incorporated into the day-to-day? What will you need to do as a facilitator to support this? When you consider these questions at the design and planning stage, you inherently build forward momentum into your meetings.

One way to do this is to end the workshop with clear next steps for each attendee – for example, create actions to follow up on, an experiment that can be reviewed in the next meeting or a question for everyone to reflect on further. This makes the difference between a well-run meeting and a well-run meeting that has an impact on the business.

The more you run these meetings effectively, the more you'll find yourself picking up the same skills that transfer directly into leading a workshop culture – the skills to facilitate a team through change and high performance. You're not just pulling a team together, you're thinking about how the team as a whole is more valuable than the sum of its parts and what you'll be able to do as a result. There is magic to be created if you get the conditions just right.

If you see your meeting rhythm as the heartbeat of your team, it is the thread that connects everything that you do. What happens in your meetings should be directly linked to what happens in between them. This enables you to look at your team's collaboration – meetings and the space in between – as an overall and connected experience. When we think about it as an experience, we see the potential for improving collaboration and how people interact within that system. That is our team culture!

TRY THIS: run your first 'workshop culture' workshop

1. Facilitate a conversation about the work you need to do and the discussions you need to have.
2. Use the purpose-outputs-questions template to explore how each of these discussions would translate into different meeting formats and how frequently you need to run them.
3. Create a draft schedule for your team's meeting rhythm using the template in Figure 7.3.

Remember to follow up by reviewing the ideas that came out of the session.

Chapter 7 – key takeaways:

- You can think about your meetings at two levels – strategically and tactically. Strategically, you can take a step back to make sure you have different meeting formats to meet different purposes. Tactically, you can ensure that what happens in each of those meetings serves its purpose.
- When your team learns facilitation skills, they are also learning key communication skills that will improve their conversations.
- By thinking about the questions we want to ask our team, we can shift our meetings to be more interactive and inclusive.

- We don't have to run all of our meetings like workshops. We can start with a few techniques, like check-ins, individual thinking and breakout groups.

We've looked at how running your meetings is an impactful process for shifting your culture – by looking at how they are facilitated to influence how your team communicates. Now it's time to look at how you design the way you work as a team to optimize your creativity and productivity. That's the focus of Chapter 8.

Chapter 8

Design –
designing ways of working

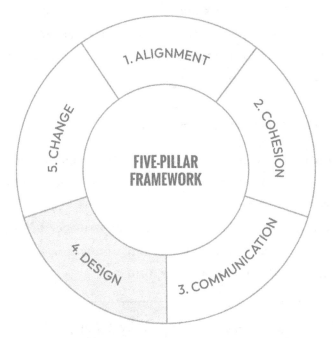

Once you've established your team's purpose, vision and values, and built more self-awareness and cohesion by understanding each other better, you will start to have more clarity on how you want to be together as a team. You'll see opportunities for improvement and start to see how some of the individual and collective habits and behaviours may be getting in the way of your full performance potential.

Here, you literally 'design'. You are now in a position to create your working methods and processes based on the team that you want to be. And like many of the aspects we have already covered, applying design to your teamwork is a skill that we can practice and cultivate. Eventually this will become the natural way that you approach your work.

In this chapter we'll look at a range of aspects for working by design as a team, such as creating routines and rituals, optimizing team productivity, asynchronous working and sharing information. We'll explore how you can remove barriers and blockers to progress so that your team can deliver to a high standard without compromising well-being and connection.

Before we dive in, think about some of the current pain points you've observed in how your team works together. What is slowing your team down and causing the most frustration? Have these challenges in mind as you work through this chapter.

By the end of this chapter, you will have learnt:

- why routines and rituals are better than 'team building'
- how you can design for team flow and to manage workload and overwhelm
- how to consider the end-to-end experience for your team's collaboration and how technology can help whether you are a remote, hybrid or co-located team.

CASE STUDY: working by design, not by default

One of the most profound transformations I've seen in a team occurred because I helped them to work by design rather than by default. It was powerful because the team, like many others, were unaware that this was a possibility for them.

The members of this particular team were relatively new to the working world – most were in their first job or just a few years into their career. They worked in an organization that was fast-moving and results-focused, and this led to a heavy workload. There was a big emphasis on individual performance.

People were keen to prove themselves and were getting pulled into new ideas and initiatives. As a result, most of the team had learnt to work reactively. They weren't being intentional about how they got their work done, because they didn't know how to be. What mattered was that they got it done and to a high standard, and inadvertently, it was what the culture encouraged.

This was impacting the way they related to each other. Many people were stressed, and sometimes short-tempered. There was little empathy across the team, and some people were suffering from burnout. Furthermore, the collective belief was that 'this is how work is'. They had no other reference points because they had never experienced anything else.

When we explored 'working by design', it was like a lightbulb turned on. Everything that they'd heard and assumed about what working life was meant to be – difficult, overwhelming, stressful – was upended. They realized they could have more power over their day than they thought. We spoke about how they could allocate time for reflection, check in with others to see how they were doing, timeblock their calendar to focus on work, be more curious about their colleagues' ways of working and run their meetings differently. It was all about creating better habits and committing to them.

Suddenly work became an opportunity to improve their own effectiveness, which they realized would also have an impact on their delivery and overall team performance. We created a collective plan for them to start shifting to being more intentional about their work and how they would stay accountable to those changes.

Team culture as a product in development

It can be a revelation for a team that they have agency over *how* they are going to work together. They are surprised by the idea that they can craft their working methods around themselves, and even be creative about it. For so many people, work is delivered on autopilot. We're pulled along by deadlines and the other demands made of us. So we get there without thinking about how to get there – we just know we need to get it done.

With our workplace and wider environment constantly changing around us and other influences impacting our work, we can get pulled in so many different directions. The more intentional we are about our working methods, the more we are likely to reach our goals. As a team, having regular conversations about *how* you collaborate is one way to support this. It's not about creating strict processes and rules that confine your team – our teams need to be as dynamic as the world we exist in. Rather it's about looking at all of the resources and knowledge you have, identifying where you want to end up, and using your creative thinking and problem-solving skills to give you the best chance of getting there. This process can be an experience that is meaningful and enjoyable for your team.

While the concept of 'designing culture' may be new to your team, as knowledge workers, you may already be familiar with some of the techniques you can use to do this. We are used to developing new ideas every day, and with a bit of tweaking, we can apply this same approach to our culture.

The makers of the productivity tool Asana view their company culture the same as they would a technology product in continuous development. They consider that it has bugs that need to be fixed (i.e. pain points) and is something to which you can apply innovative thinking to solve.[1] When you consider it like this, there are a number of tools you can use to design your culture, which make it an engaging team activity, and will help you to differentiate your team and highlight its unique characteristics.

Prototype and experiment with your culture

In Chapter 4, we introduced how you can use design thinking techniques to consider yourself and your team as 'users' of your working experience. I shared a brief description of the discover, define, develop and deliver stages of the Double Diamond. Here I want to expand more on the final stage – deliver – and on the idea of *prototyping*.

When you are prototyping, you are creating an experiment, and this may be a radical idea to many teams. It means taking a more fluid approach to your working methods and engaging in ongoing learning so that you can discover what is effective. When the whole team is aware that you are all *testing* a new way of working, you encourage psychological safety and an open mindset towards continuous improvement.

TRY THIS: Double Diamond for your team

Run a short brainstorming session with your team to identify all of the areas that prevent them from doing great work. Ask them to identify the area that is causing the most challenge *and* one that is within their control to change.

Facilitate them through the Double Diamond – discover, define, develop, deliver to create a solution that you might experiment with:

1. **Discover:** what are all the pains associated with this challenge?
2. **Define:** what is the true problem that you want to solve?
3. **Develop:** what are some potential solutions for working differently?
4. **Deliver:** what solution could you experiment and try first?

Designing routines and rituals over 'team building'

Why team building is no longer enough

When was the last time you arranged a team-building activity and what did it look like? Often, team building is seen as something that happens separately from work. Team-building events may be held annually and have a heavy focus on socializing – doing non-work activities. Some may even involve competitive games. These activities can provide much-needed time for the team to bond away from their work. The aim is to build camaraderie to make collaboration easier (although some research has shown that these activities can have a negative effect if they are truly not voluntary).[2] The things that team building aims to achieve – better relationships and stronger connections with our colleagues – are all aspects that we need regularly in our work. So why not bring some of that intention into our everyday?

In a workshop culture, we aim for routines and rituals rather than 'team building'. These routines and rituals are weaved into the actual work your team is doing, so they have the outcome of 'building the team' in a more natural, integrated way. Team-building events can still happen, but they shouldn't be the only time where you pay attention to social connection.

How routines and rituals support team culture

Changing to a new way of working doesn't happen by itself. First, we set the intention for what we want to do. Then we need to find ways of adopting new behaviours that reflect that intention in our work. This is where routines and rituals come in.

Routines and rituals are designed to create connection, communication and collaboration. They are structures that achieve a certain outcome, and when performed regularly, they start to become new embedded behaviours and habits (which we'll look at in detail in Chapter 9). A routine and a ritual are slightly different but can also crossover.

A routine is a series of actions stitched together. Your team likely already has some routines, such as your regular meetings, the rhythm of your meetings, or what happens in those meetings. Consider it like a dance routine – actions performed one after the other. Routines are often systemized to keep things going in the right direction. They are about process, and feel relatively automatic.

A ritual has more social meaning attached and is designed to connect people, get people into a certain way of thinking or to mark an occasion. If you have team methods that serve a specific purpose – for example, closing or marking the end of a project, acknowledging someone for their good work, presenting a team award or celebrating team birthdays – then these are rituals. They also form an important part of a team's identity. In *Rituals for Work: 50 Ways to Create Engagement, Shared Purpose and a Culture That Can Adapt to Change*, Ozenc and Hagan say of rituals: 'They are practices that can bond people together, help us move through conflicts, amp us up to better performances, and assist us in adapting to change.'[3]

We can take the principles of both routines and rituals and incorporate them directly into our team work. For example, a workshop can be seen as a routine if it is a regular session that you run, like a weekly goal-setting session or monthly review. A retrospective can be an end of project routine to extract learnings for next time. Alternatively, the activities within a workshop could be a series of mini-rituals within that one session. A check-in at the start of a workshop or a check-out at the end are examples of rituals that have a purpose – to transition into a collective space or to close down your time together. Or, the workshop can be a full ritual in itself if it has a more social purpose. A post-mortem at the end of a project, for example, can also celebrate completion.

Why develop routines and rituals?

As well as helping us to strengthen our team culture, there are also other benefits that routines and rituals have:

Integration: They serve the purpose of finding an accessible way to turn our desired behaviours into action. We repeat them over and over until they become part of our team identity. A great way of making team values real is to translate them into routines and rituals that your team performs together so that they become seamlessly integrated into the way you 'do things'.

Reducing cognitive load: We have a certain amount of capacity – called cognitive load – to hold information in our working memory, which is about ten items of information at a time.[4] Research suggests that 'heavy cognitive load may have negative implications on the work performance'.[5] So if we reduce the amount of information we hold in our working memory, we can create more capacity for other tasks, including higher-level thinking tasks such as creativity, problem-solving and critical thinking. When we create routines and rituals, we free up the need to remember actions by translating them into more automatic behaviours.

Creating safety and familiarity: Rituals create familiarity for a team, especially in times of uncertainty. They form a known behaviour that people can come back to when experiencing a lot of change and disruption. This helps a team to stay grounded and connected – there is safety in creating a common social currency.

When we ritualize workshop activities and bring them into our work, it becomes who we are as a team, not just when we get together for an away day. Good routines and rituals enable us to practice the elements of collaboration until they become regular behaviour.

Optimizing team productivity – what design can address

Team flow – the ultimate aim

We long for extended periods of time where we can go deep into a challenge, uninterrupted, using the best of our abilities and enjoying it as we do so. Sadly, this is not the reality for many of us in today's workplaces. Our calendars are punctuated with meetings; we have a steady stream of emails dropping into our inboxes and constant pings from our team messaging tools.

The concept of 'flow' was coined by psychologist Mihaly Csikszentmihalyi and has become a commonly referenced concept, particularly in the realm of creativity.[6] Flow brings challenge, deep engagement, focus and great work in a way that is fulfilling. It is often considered the highest level of performance, and achieving it is the holy grail for many knowledge workers. It has business benefits too – companies see higher levels of engagement and productivity when their workers are able to achieve flow.[7]

While most research on flow relates to the individual, *group flow* was explored by Keith Sawyer in his 2015 paper 'Group Flow and Group Genius'. He describes conditions of group flow in the following way: 'In group flow, participants must feel in control, yet at the same time, they must remain flexible, listen closely, and always be willing to defer to the emergent flow of the group. The most innovative teams are the ones that can manage that paradox.'[8]

Sawyer established group flow's nine key principles as group goals, close listening, complete concentration, being in control, blending egos, equal participation, knowing team mates, good communication and being progress-oriented.[9] So, in striving towards a workshop culture, you are already creating the conditions for group flow to happen.

The concept was researched further in 2016 by van den Hout et al. who described *team flow* as a 'situation in which all the team members are completely involved in their common activities as part of a collaboration toward the common purpose'.[10] According to their research, team flow can happen at three levels: (1) an individual experiencing flow when delivering a task as part of a team; (2) a team member gets energy from the team dynamic; or (3) the team have a shared energy, reflecting a common state of flow.[11]

There are various ways that you can consider group or team flow. So how do we achieve it?

Designing for team flow – learning from workshops

A workshop is a great opportunity to observe group or team flow – where the participants are fully engaged and operating at optimum levels of performance together. A facilitator will often design a session to achieve this. We want participants to feel as if time is going quickly; we want them to get into 'the zone' and to produce great work. We want harmony balanced with productive conflict, creative breakthroughs and little surprises that momentarily take us in a different direction.

To achieve this, facilitators have a clear purpose and will design the process based on this. They will set out how a team will spend their time together and gently orientate them towards the finish point. We may highlight connections from an objective view that the team may not see, and we celebrate everyone on the team. We create the right environment (through facilitation), and then we get out of the way. We have a framework and keep the end goal in mind, but hold that lightly when the team comes together so that they can make their own mark. We can take all of those elements and design ways of working to recreate this in our team within the context of a workshop culture.

Think about what flow might look like for your team. Bring together all the knowledge you have about your team so far – the vision and values you've created together, and what you've learnt about how individuals do their best work. Based on what your team needs to deliver and how you define high performance, when might be good to optimize for team flow. What could you aim to do together in those times?

Managing overwhelm and redesigning workloads

We can also use a design approach to help us manage and assess our workloads. If you feel your team is overwhelmed and too busy, take some time to understand the work you are collectively doing so that you can reprioritize and reorganize. Bring your team together to review your purpose and what you need to deliver. Grab some sticky notes – real or virtual – and get your team to individually 'braindump' all of the areas and tasks they are responsible for onto a shared white-board. Come back as a full group and start to arrange those individual tasks into themes, as shown in Figure 8.1. This will give you a sense of the breadth of work your team is doing and has remit for. You will get a good overview of whether the capacity and resources of your team cover their commitments and responsibilities.

Make sure you have a common definition of 'high performance' and a collective agreement as to what is important. This definition will depend on your team's context. Set these standards together, and while you are free to exceed them, you will still have a clear baseline for what is expected.

At this point you can also discuss any overlaps, duplication and redundant tasks, and pinpoint any major concerns. You can reset your priorities as a team and generate ideas for how you will manage your workload going forward, based on what you have agreed.

Having this laid out in front of you, with clear and realistic expec-tations, sets your team up with the best chances of finding your flow together. It becomes more powerful when paired with visibility and transparency of tasks and information.

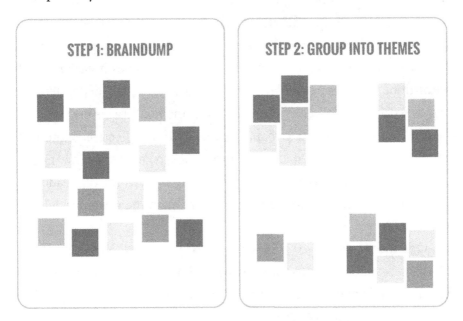

Figure 8.1 Braindump exercise.

TRY THIS: task braindump

If your team is feeling overwhelmed, encourage them each to braindump everything they are working on. Work together to create a common agreement for 'high performance' – which is your common expectations for quality, delivery and success measures – and then reset your priorities.

Transparent information to support the flow of work

How much time is lost in your day by trying to find files or get updates? Have your team members ever wasted time by duplicating the work of someone else? This time spent trying to find information sucks energy away from the valuable creative thinking that can set teams apart. It's not just that we have too much to do, but that we are doing it inefficiently.

As we have seen, autonomy and freedom are important within a workshop culture – this creates engagement and motivation. However, the exchange for this is open and clear communication. More flexibility requires a deeper level of trust, and this can be supported by transparency. In some cases it may even feel necessary to 'over communicate', so that information flows in a way that makes it easier to get work done. This is particularly important if there are dependencies across work. Transparency of tasks in a team encourages everyone to be more accountable. They manage capacity more effectively amongst themselves, avoid bottlenecks and offer help to colleagues that might be overwhelmed. It takes sole responsibility away from the leader as the conduit of information, and empowers team members by putting it into their hands.

One tool to visualize tasks is the kanban board (Figure 8.2) which divides a team's work into three areas: what they need *to do*, what they are *doing* and what has been *done*. It's a simple way to ensure everyone is aware of what's happening.

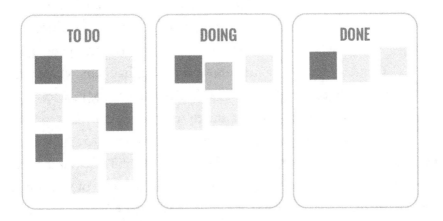

Figure 8.2 Kanban board.

Many online team-productivity tools are designed to optimize transparency. They ensure that tasks and information don't get lost or duplicated, and aim to keep a team on the same page. However, these tools are only as powerful as the individuals using them. Everyone must develop a bias (and habit) for sharing and open communication, and appreciate the value that this ultimately brings to their work.

Designing connection

Time alone, time together and asynchronous working

Great collaboration is creating a balance between, and benefiting from, both individual and collective expertise. Our times together in meetings keep us in sync; and then there are times when we are working alone. In the same way we design our meetings, we also have an opportunity to design the spaces in between our collaborative sessions, considering how they also support our overall team effectiveness and performance. We can look at the whole 'lifecycle' for which a team will work together and design the entire experience – the times together, times apart, co-creating, working independently – from beginning to end.

The more technical term for the 'spaces in between' is *asynchronous working*. The conversation around asynchronous working has grown considerably with the rise of remote, hybrid and geographically distributed teams. Asynchronous working happens when team members need to contribute to the same piece of work or project, yet it is not necessary, or even possible due to time zones, for them to work at exactly the same time (synchronously). Team members have more flexibility over when they will make their contributions, and many workers are starting to express a preference for this way of working as a result. In 2023, according to a research survey from Miro (the collaboration software), nearly three-quarters of knowledge workers believe that adopting asynchronous working effectively would improve their culture.[12]

As with many aspects within a workshop culture, there is an opportunity to optimize asynchronous working for collective team input, particularly when it follows an intense period of collaborative, synchronous work and precedes another, as Figure 8.3 shows.

Figure 8.3 Designing for asynchronous and synchronous work.

To coordinate asynchronous work effectively, it's important to set expectations. Following meetings or workshops, be clear about what people need to contribute by when, to what quality and in what format. To keep momentum going, regularly check in with team members on their tasks so that they continue to feel connected. And, of course, keep using dedicated team collaboration tools to communicate. The reframing of asynchronous work matters too. Emphasize that this is part of an overall collaborative experience, rather a secondary, less important part of our teamwork.

Remote and hybrid teams

The workshop culture framework is applicable regardless of how you are located as a team – in office, remote or hybrid. But here are a few additional things to consider based on how your team is organized:

- If your team is fully remote, you need to be *more* intentional about maintaining connection and communication and creating a clear team identity and culture. For example, annual in-person team retreats may form an important part of your meeting rhythm.
- If you have a hybrid team, you need to specify when you will spend time physically together (not just the number of days you will be in the office) and, if possible, schedule it in. Then design what you will do together in those times.
- Some team members may even value being in the presence of others when they are working on their individual tasks (this may be a way of achieving team flow as we discussed earlier). Arranging remote or in-person 'co-working' sessions may meet this need, where you come together for a specific period of time for mutual accountability.
- All types of teams should consider when they will work synchronously or asynchronously, and how you will connect as a team within and around those moments.

Any kind of remote working means staying mindful of recreating the elements that might naturally occur in an office – for example, reaching out to a colleague for an informal chat, taking breaks together or serendipitous meetings. These social interactions need to be designed as routines and rituals so that remote team members maintain a sense of connection.

A word about technology

Naturally our teams will use a number of digital tools to communicate, share information and store content – they have transformed the way we get work done and collaborate. We also need to be mindful of how we use these platforms, and ensure they enhance and support our ways of working rather than becoming an obstruction. Remember the challenge of 'collaborative overload' that we mentioned in Chapter 6? Sometimes the very tools that are designed to help us optimize our work may also be unproductively increasing our workloads.

These tools are powerful and useful, yet they are created to meet the needs of a wide range of teams rather than yours specifically. So once you have explored how your team will work together, you also have the opportunity to design how you will use these tools to work within the context of your team. Avoid using them by default without having a conversation about how they will support your work – for example, when is it more appropriate for you to use instant messaging or group chat rather than email? How will you use your project management system, and what is a consistent process for organizing your shared files? This may feel granular, but it is one of those times when a little thought upfront can be a gamechanger for productivity and progress further down the line. It can be the difference in helping your team to find information quickly and avoid miscommunication.

Chapter 8 – key takeaways:

- Being intentional about your team's collaboration methods can change their experience of work.
- You can use the Double Diamond to help your team ideate and develop new ways of working.

- Routines and rituals help us stay connected as a team by turning intention into behaviour, reducing cognitive load and creating a sense of familiarity.
- Making tasks visible can help with workloads, reduce confusion and duplication, and increase accountability in your team.
- The spaces in between our collaborative moments – when we are working asynchronously – are just as important, and they can also be designed.

In this chapter we covered some practical methods to design new ways of working. While some of these techniques may be new to you and your team now, the more you do them, the more they will become central to the way that you work. In order to see the transformation, you'll need to make sure these changes stick. That's what we'll focus on next.

Chapter 9

Change – continuous improvement

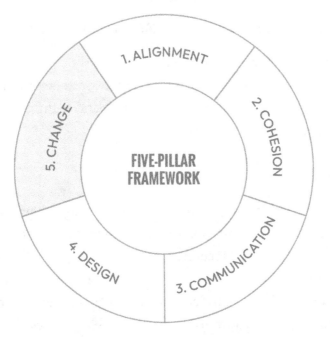

The final pillar of the workshop culture framework is Change. It is focused on how your team will implement new behaviours to transform your culture. Without this pillar, many of the ideas we've discussed up until now will remain as theory. The impact comes in translating those ideas into day-to-day action and creating an environment of continuous improvement.

In this chapter we'll introduce some key concepts and practical tools to facilitate and sustain change. We'll also consider some additional elements, such as coaching and skills development, that will support your team's transformation towards a workshop culture.

By the end of this chapter you will have learnt how to:

- evolve team habits so that they support your performance
- make collective change in your team more manageable
- involve your team in making commitments and increase accountability.

CASE STUDY: make tiny tweaks, not sweeping changes

As a reminder of the fourth principle of workshop culture – 'make tiny tweaks, not sweeping changes' – here are some examples of teams that converted their intention for a better culture into real-life behaviours with a tiny first step.

Say hello

A client had decided on 'we are considerate' as one of their company values, and realized that this meant exemplifying a more caring culture internally. They identified that one of the simple things they could do was to say 'hello' to each other as they came into the office in the morning. To an outsider, this seems like a tiny action, and it is. But for a company that wasn't used to doing this, even just the recognition that this was important created a new collective awareness amongst the senior team. They realized that shifting to this habitual behaviour would have a significant impact on how employees started their days.

Creative nudges

One team wanted to explore opportunities for bringing more everyday creativity into their culture. I introduced them to a range of ideation techniques and helped them to develop their own methods for sparking new thinking. But we also knew they needed a way to remember these techniques when work got busy.

I started off by sending them regular nudges on their chat platform, at the start and end of each week, as reminders to incorporate them into their work. After a short while, they continued with these prompts themselves.

Fifteen minutes a week

A busy, central team in an organization were often in firefighting mode. They were being brought into 'urgent and important' issues that disrupted their day. However, they wanted to be seen more as consultants and thought partners to their internal clients. This meant they needed to spend more time on 'important but not urgent' topics (remember the Eisenhower Matrix in Chapter 4?). A series of workshops provided the space for them to discuss their service at a higher level – how their work was connected, the value they provided and the identity they wanted to form as a team. After these workshops, the team committed to creating this space intentionally for themselves. The leader created a recurring 15-minute weekly-meeting invite, which everyone then used to reflect on their own professional development.

A new approach to change

A workshop is just the start

A core theme throughout this book is that in a workshop culture, work doesn't end when the workshop does. Your team may experience breakthroughs, build great ideas and have a mindset shift in a workshop. However, the true impact is when you see all of that manifest for the team when they are back in their regular work.

A team may take the step to run a workshop to 'improve their culture', hoping that the transformation will happen in a three-hour session. While it can certainly kickstart the process, there is still work that needs to happen afterwards to sustain the momentum and adapt some of their existing patterns. Behaviour change sounds simple in theory but is challenging in practice. How many of us have set new intentions for a more productive, healthier habit, but have failed to make them last? I'm guessing a very high number! To make changes stick, we need a good understanding of how we shift our current habits.

A facilitator knows that while a workshop is a key catalyst to change, it is also just the beginning of the conversation. Generating new or different ideas in a workshop that are to be implemented means *doing* something new or different, too. Everyone must be committed to making the necessary change, otherwise those ideas stay as a concept.

Changing team habits

We all have our own *individual habits* and ways that we approach our work. This might be our communication styles, productivity routines and other personal rhythms. We also have ways that we tend to interact with others – how we give and receive feedback, the way we write emails and how we share information. These are like *collaboration habits*; in other words the way that you naturally work with others. When we become aware of our individual and collaboration habits, we can share these with our team. We explored various ways to discover and discuss this in Chapter 6 – the Cohesion pillar.

Your team will also have habits – *team habits* – which reflect the way that you work together. These are the actions that you and your team perform time and time again – whether conscious or unconscious. It could be the tone of how you talk to each other, the way you share information, the types of meetings you hold, what happens during them, and many other aspects of how you interact with each other. It's the way you *do things*. Think about the way that you communicate. Does your team default to picking up the phone, sending an email or pinging on Slack? It may seem that these approaches are universal, but these are all the habits you have developed when working together, and they make up your unique team culture.

- Individual habits = how you personally get work done.
- Collaboration habits = how you interact with others.
- Team habits = how you act as a team.

The key to high performance is to identify your team habits and ensure they positively contribute to team productivity, motivation and engagement. For example, if your team members have the habit of sending terse Slack messages when they are frustrated, aim to replace this with a habit where they respond with a question that comes from genuine curiosity. If everyone committed to this small shift in behaviour, it would change the atmosphere dramatically. Set yourselves the challenge, over the course of a few days, of observing your tendencies without blame or judgement. This could be the way you speak to each other, how you communicate information and the reactions you have as you interact. You may find it useful to speak one-on-one with members of your team so that they can share the collective behaviours – both good and bad – that they notice.

Change is a process, not an event

Another misjudgement we make about change is that the journey to becoming a high-performing team has an end point, and once we get across the finish line we are done. As we explored in Chapter 4, we need to look at change as a continuous process instead.

When you've taken the first steps to building a workshop culture, and your team is moving forward, the work to sustain it is ongoing. High-performing teams are those that proactively and continuously improve the way they work. They are constantly identifying opportunities to tweak and optimize their performance. High-performing teams see change as the fabric of what they do, not something that happens occasionally.

Our team habits can develop without us realizing it, but ideally, we will design our habits for the behaviours and outcomes that we want. These are also not fixed, so we should regularly review and tweak them, as shown in Figure 9.1, as well as ensuring any unproductive habits haven't slipped into our way of working.

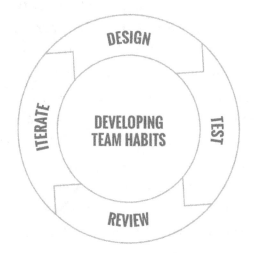

Figure 9.1 Developing team habits.

In their 2014 research paper, Chatman et al. showed that technology firms with the highest financial performance have a strong sense of the behaviours and habits they need to achieve their goals, but they also stay adaptable so that they can exist successfully within a dynamic environment.[1] While a team needs an intentional approach to their culture and to be clear on their desired habits, they must also adapt those ways of working based on what is happening around them.

Change is hard, so we need to manage it

We know that we are more likely to achieve a change in behaviour when we set a clear goal, yet changing our behaviour doesn't end there.

Although we know what success may look like, we also need to shift our ingrained habits. Intention, memory and willpower alone isn't enough, and so we need to be proactive about how we will change.

Change is hard because of the effort it takes to proactively shift to new behaviours. Those behaviours may be beneficial to us in the long term, but they are harder to do in the short term. It's much easier to default to our automatic ways of being, even if this is not serving us. Neuroscience tells us that each habit we have has a neural pathway,[2] and when we create a new habit, we are forming a new one. Our brains literally need to be rewired! It's more than saying we'll just change our behaviour. We also need to explore *how*.

Managing change is a balance between making the end goal compelling enough to kickstart the process and making the actions to get there as frictionless as possible. We need to set ourselves up for success and then hold ourselves accountable to make sure we stay on track. When we have lofty ambitions for high performance and innovation, the lure of instant, wide-scale change might seem juicy, but the first most effective step is often a small step. A large goal like 'better collaboration' has to be broken down into smaller actions to make it easy to put into practice. Sustainable change takes small shifts and is built into your approach as a team.

Understanding behaviour change

The psychology of change

Much has been written about behaviour change, all backed by extensive research. Here are a few key concepts that can help us in our teams.

Don't rely on willpower. Setting an intention isn't enough, and while we may believe willpower is all we need, it plays a smaller part than we think. Self-control has been shown to act like a muscle – we start our day with a lot in our reserve, and it gradually diminishes as we make more decisions and exert more mental energy throughout the day.[3] This means that if we have a particularly difficult day at work, or are working on a challenging project, we will allocate energy to what is demanding our attention rather than the new habits we want to develop. That's why we often revert to 'bad' habits under pressure or stress. So we need to create clear reminders of the new behaviours we want to develop in our team.

Context is important. Habits don't exist in a vacuum. Our behaviour is influenced by what is around us. As James Clear explores in *Atomic Habits: An Easy and Proven Way to Build Good Habits and Break Bad Ones*, 'visual cues are the greatest catalyst of our behaviour'.[4] What we can see in our environment can make it more likely or less likely for us to perform an action. This can be as simple as checking our emails each time a notification pops up, or deactivating those notifications so that we don't get distracted. So what are we crafting in our environment, physical or virtual, to make it more likely for us to perform the actions that we want?

Small changes build momentum. One method for reducing the friction to behaviour change is to break a larger goal into an initial tiny action that edges us in the right direction. BJ Fogg, pioneer of Tiny Habits®, encourages us to make the first step of a new habit as small as possible – even minuscule – and perform it repeatedly so that we break down that initial barrier.[5] As that first step becomes easier, we become more familiar with the behaviour. Then we can gradually extend it until we have built the full habit. For example, a goal to share more ideas with each other might start with each team member simply making a note to find something that inspires them each day and capturing it somewhere for themselves. After a couple of weeks, you might encourage them to share it with one other team member and then eventually the whole team. Finally, you might set up a part of a regular meeting where you openly discuss and critique all of the new ideas you gathered.

Consistency is key. 'Grand gestures' can have a big one-off impact but can be short-lived. Doing something little and often becomes more embedded as a natural behaviour than doing something big, less frequently. In *Atomic Habits*, James Clear advocates for 'habit tracking' a process where we aim to create an unbroken streak for a habit we do regularly.[6] It creates momentum and encourages us to keep going. In your team, could you visually recreate the idea of habit tracking in a shared space, so that team members can check off each time they have performed a new behaviour they want to build?

Reward and feedback loops. We are more likely to stay committed to a new habit if we know there will be an immediate reward and positive reinforcement. The 'habit loop', as shared by Charles Duhigg in *The Power of Habit: Why We Do What We Do and How to Change*, illustrates how habits become reinforced when we repeatedly go through the cycle of 'cue (or trigger), routine and reward'.[7] For our teams, part of the reward is knowing that the change we have implemented is making a difference. As it's sometimes only possible to see the impact when looking back over a period of time, we also need to make sure we stop in to check on progress regularly. You can bring these check-ins to the routines or rituals you develop.

Habit stacking. We can increase our success of remembering a new habit if we attach it to something we are already doing – an existing behaviour acts as a cue for a new one. This is called stacking.[8] This might look like bringing a new activity into an existing meeting rather than creating a whole new meeting entirely. Or ending a meeting five minutes early so that everyone can take some time to reflect on their week.

The role of motivation in change

How do you ensure your team is motivated to change? Ryan and Deci's paper on 'self-determination theory' pioneered our understanding of the role of motivation in behaviour change, identifying competence, autonomy, and relatedness as key factors[9] (this paper was a key influence for Daniel Pink's book, *Drive*, which we referenced earlier in Chapter 5).

Competence relates to how challenging a task is to complete – not too easy that we get bored, not too difficult that we get frustrated. Autonomy (as we've covered extensively throughout this book) relates to us being able to perform the task in our own way and having control over its completion. Finally, relatedness is how connected we feel to the task – do we understand why it is necessary and our role in achieving it?

The workshop culture framework starts with the Alignment pillar – creating a strong vision and purpose for your team to align around, and creating team values that help us stay connected to that vision. This comes back full circle in our final pillar – Change – as a way of underpinning the rationale for behaviour change. Without this clear direction, ultimately any attempt to shift habits will be even more challenging.

Team behaviour change – collective implementation intentions

Another concept to consider for your team behaviour change is collective implementation intention.

Implementation intention is a concept that takes goal setting one step further. It demonstrates that when we are specific about when, how and where we will perform a new action and we specify how we will counteract any barriers, a new action is more likely to stick.[10] This is described as an 'if-then' statement. Most of the research around implementation intentions focus on the individual, but they are also impactful at the team level. Collective implementation intentions are set, collectively, with a team agreeing to how they will respond if a situation occurs ('If we encounter situation Y, then we will show response X!').[11]

For example, in your team, you might agree to a new 30-minute inspiration session on a Tuesday morning to share any new insights from the previous week, but stating that if someone has an urgent client deadline, instead they will share a one-line update in your shared project space.

Tools and techniques to initiate and sustain change

From start-stop-continue to continue-stop-start

A simple exercise for your team to explore the habits that they want to build is the start-stop-continue framework, a variation of the SKS (stop-keep-start) method developed by Phil Daniels.[12] Start-stop-continue is a straightforward and popular tool for end of project reviews. In the context of behaviour change, I feel it works better when flipped around to continue-stop-start:

Continue covers what you are already doing as a team that works. This is affirming your strengths and what you can maintain. There is no behaviour change here, just a reinforcement of existing habits. This is where you will experience the least or no friction.

Stop will take slightly more energy because you and your team will need to become aware of the behaviours you no longer want to do, and make a conscious effort to stop yourself. This may be about changing your process or environment to make it less likely that you will default to these behaviours, or perhaps playfully calling each other out when you see it.

Start is where most of the work of behaviour change happens. These are habits and behaviours that your team are not currently doing but you know would benefit you if you were to adopt them. If you've taken your team through the Double Diamond exercise in Chapter 8, it may be the ideas that emerge in the 'deliver' phase. These new ideas take the most energy and are where we need to be most disciplined.

The path of least resistance

From the 'start' phase of the continue-stop-start model, identify the ideas that would initially be the easiest to implement but for which you are likely to see results quite quickly. The impact effort matrix, developed by Bjørn Andersen, Tom Fagerhaug and Marti Beltz, is a tool that helps you to plot ideas based on exactly that – the amount of effort they would take and the level of impact they will have.[13] For example, introducing a new digital app might help your team to organize your ideas more effectively, but researching the range of options available, choosing one, putting it in place and then learning how to use it will take a lot of energy. This might be a longer-term project. In contrast, asking everyone to drop their top key learning from the week into a group-chat thread is something you could do straight away and would instantly get your team sharing new information. This is what the impact effort matrix identifies as 'quick wins'.

Facilitate a conversation with your team about where you might arrange some of your new ideas for team habits, behaviours and actions on the matrix and challenge each other on the true impact they will make and the effort they will require. Also consider what other factors might prevent you from putting any new ideas into practice, and discuss how you can remove those barriers.

An exercise like this can also form the start of your team culture roadmap, where you build a timeline for your development and regularly review your progress. These conversations continue to build your muscle for change, all starting with experimentation. You can then reflect and iterate based on what you've learnt and start the process again.

Micro-actions and reflection

Each time you meet as a team, particularly to run 'workshop culture' workshops (see Chapter 7), encourage everyone to commit to a small action that they will try before you next come together again. Remember to use some of the principles we've covered in this chapter – for example, collective implementation intention, keeping new actions small and fostering consistency – so that your team can increase their chances of success.

You will naturally have varying results as to who will be able to stick to their commitment. For those that do, invite them to share what's happened as a result. This will reinforce their efforts and help them to embed the behaviour further. For those that were not able to stick to their commitment, get curious about why that was to understand more about your team:

- Was it a lack of time?
- Was the task too big and difficult to do?
- Is it actually important, or is there something else that could be more impactful?

Reflecting on and learning from what happens when someone is not able to stick to a commitment (as long as it doesn't become a pattern) can be useful information for identifying and removing barriers. Aim to maintain this cycle of committing to micro-actions and reflecting on them to build more self-awareness in your team and encourage continuous improvement.

Systems to sustain change

Team culture development is a new capability that many of us have to train ourselves for. There are a range of techniques we can use to keep it a priority:

Nudges and reminders: When we have a compelling vision for our team, which we translate into our values and then into behaviours, these can be expressed as micro-actions, as we just covered. We can create nudges and reminders to keep these micro-actions top of mind to subtly shift us in the right direction. This can be as simple as creating an email – scheduled or manual – with a question prompt, or a calendar invite that pops up as a notification. Or, as demonstrated in the case study at the beginning of this chapter, as a question on your chat platform.

Making activity visible: For a team, having visibility of your collective goals, as well as tracking contributions, can be a powerful way to demonstrate accountability. You can create shared spaces – a virtual or physical whiteboard, dashboard or counter system – that shows how many times someone has performed a new habit. Combine this with the idea of streaks, and we can encourage gentle competition between team members. Remember to celebrate team members' activity when they've stayed accountable.

Integrate regular conversations into work: Make sure to reinforce these interventions with regular conversations about progress and what people are experiencing through the change in your team meetings. Your team will learn from experimenting with new ideas in the real world as they come up against challenges in their daily work.

Testing, iteration and continuous improvement: These systems set the foundation to make change the fabric of your team. Experimentation becomes part of your culture, which builds an open mindset, psychological safety and a bias for reflection. This will gradually filter into other aspects of your work as you create an upward spiral in your team for more agility, adaptability and resilience.

TRY THIS: shifting into new team behaviours

1. Facilitate a continue-stop-start exercise with your team to identify your existing habits and ones you want to introduce.
2. Plot any new habits or behaviours that you'd like to 'start' on an impact effort matrix.

3. When you've identified your 'quick wins', ask everyone to commit to a micro-action to shift that behaviour forward.
4. Set up a reminder to send a gentle nudge for everyone to share how they're progressing.

Building a workshop culture – a blended approach to change

The framework

We've now explored the whole five-pillar framework that supports you in your journey towards a workshop culture. This framework is underpinned by four key foundations to support the approach:

1. Workshops are more than a one-off event.
2. Maintain a constant balance between creativity and productivity.
3. Make tiny tweaks, not sweeping changes.
4. A workshop culture is designed.

Before anything, your team will need to adopt a growth mindset and believe it is possible to improve the way you work together as a team. The five-pillar framework helps you to spot where there are opportunities to transform your culture. It is not a step-by-step process, but a way of identifying where you most need to put your attention:

1. **Alignment:** look at the big picture and identify your team vision and values. Be clear on your team's purpose, everything you need to *do* and how you need to *be* to achieve your goals.
2. **Cohesion:** build self-awareness and empathy by exploring and discussing the diversity of expertise and ways of working within your team. This is part of your unique team culture.
3. **Communication:** explore how facilitation skills can help you all relate to each other more effectively, particularly, but not exclusively, in your meetings.

4. **Design:** consider the different ways of working along with routines and rituals that you can put in place to keep your team connected, aligned, creative and productive throughout your work.

5. **Change:** understand your team's habits and build approaches for making a commitment to change, staying accountable and regularly reviewing your progress.

Keep coming back to this framework, particularly when your team has experienced a change – a team member joins or leaves, the nature of work that you're doing changes (e.g. a new client or initiative) or something in your wider environment shifts.

Developing transferable skills

The focus of a workshop culture is on how your team changes the way they work. However, a secondary outcome is the skills they develop as a result. These include:

- strategic thinking
- creative thinking, problem-solving and ideation
- goal setting
- reflection and self-awareness
- empathy
- feedback and difficult conversations
- facilitation and meeting design
- active listening
- communication
- productivity and time management
- planning and scheduling
- design thinking
- behaviour change.

These are transferable skills that are valuable across any role, team and project. A workshop culture can transform someone's approach to work and help them to become a better collaborator, therefore improving their opportunities for career growth and development.

Supporting your team – the difference between workshops and coaching

A team that undergoes a transformation, however gradual, will impact the individuals in the team. The process of change can be challenging, as you'll be surfacing unproductive habits and reforming the way your team works. As we saw in Chapter 4, sometimes it may even feel like it gets worse before it gets better! The conversations you have, reflection you do and feedback you offer may lead a team member to become more aware of their deep-rooted habits and approaches that may be preventing their own and the team's development.

Facilitated workshops will open this up more than a usual meeting, but as they are focused on forward momentum, there is still a limit to what they can cover. Sometimes there is a need to slow down so that the emotions and feelings that are emerging can be processed while a culture is shifting.

Additional coaching conversations – both individual and team-based – can help your team to navigate and break through these blocks, delve into conflicts or tensions that might arise as they do this work, help them build self-awareness and consider how they are showing up in the team.

Creating a plan for team culture development

How will you stay committed to team culture development?

You might start with a dedicated plan or roadmap to keep you accountable and focused. Then as your team becomes more familiar with discussing your culture, you will find opportunities to connect it to other areas of your work – your annual strategic plan, team training or individual development plans.

At the start of your team's journey to a workshop culture, these conversations will be new and unfamiliar. However, the long-term goal is to eventually embed this into your ways of working and practices so that it defines your identity as a team. It's what will differentiate you and keep you growing together.

TRY THIS: create your team culture roadmap

Gather all ideas that you and your team have for improving your team culture, and start to build a timeline. What could you do:

- in the next week?
- in the next month?
- in the next three months?
- over the next few quarters, selecting a theme for each?

Remember to make your goals small and achievable, and create check-in points to review your progress.

Chapter 9 – key takeaways:

- Developing team habits is a continuous process of designing, testing, reviewing and iterating.
- We can make change more manageable by breaking it down into small actions and ensuring we: create reminders, change our environment, take consistent action and review progress.
- Start with new team habits that will be easy to implement, and you will see quick results that will help build momentum.
- The cycle of micro-actions and reflection helps to embed a culture of continuous improvement.

- We can support our team culture transformation by offering coaching, by emphasizing skills development and by making a clear roadmap for change.

The final pillar of our framework, with reference to building a workshop culture, is Change. But as we explored at the start of the book, we are operating in an uncertain and changing environment. The topics we have covered in this chapter will also help your team to stay responsive, be adaptive and build resilience.

Conclusion

Workshops are a powerful format that have the potential to transform the way we work together. We've explored how creating a workshop culture can solve some of the root causes of ineffective collaboration in our modern organizations – bad meetings, lack of engagement and lack of purpose – and help us create more creative and productive teams.

A workshop culture helps us get comfortable with the abstract nature of creativity, yet balance it with productivity to achieve high performance. It encourages us to use design to make small tweaks and changes to embed a mindset of continuous improvement in our teams.

A workshop culture can happen at the level of your team, even if it isn't common practice across an entire organization. This requires taking responsibility for the factors that you can control and influence, one of which is how you work together as a team. It enables your team to create amazing value together, which ripples out to impact those you interact with – both internal and external stakeholders – who will also benefit from your more effective ways of working, clear communication and empathy.

And it doesn't stop there. A workshop culture has further potential to positively impact our working lives and businesses. Here are some ideas to consider:

Attracting and retaining talent

One of the main reasons that people leave their jobs for self-employment is to have more freedom, flexibility and autonomy, despite the uncertainty this may bring. A workshop culture creates flexibility within a supportive structure so that people can have more control over how they work. It gives leaders the tools to create this environment, potentially creating much more attractive workplaces where people want to stay.

More diverse and inclusive workplaces

A workshop culture has a big emphasis on celebrating and valuing the unique contribution of each team member. Teams design their ways of working by balancing individual needs with the collective goal. This means we can consider different requirements – for example, for working parents and those managing health conditions – and also be conscious of the nuances that come with race, gender, age and other diverse characteristics. By bringing people's identities to the centre, we can create the culture from there, rather than forcing anyone to conform into a rigid structure that doesn't suit them. This starts to create a more welcoming and inclusive workplace for people from all walks of life.

Supporting good mental health and well-being

As more people start to suffer from burnout, caused by overwhelming workloads and toxic workplaces, we need a new approach to mental health and well-being.

We tend to see work as something that is 'energy-depleting'. We work hard and then take time away to recharge, or even recover. What if we were to see the potential of work for being 'energy-giving' instead? Something that fulfils and nourishes us. We still value time away from work to refresh ourselves, but it meets a different purpose.

With a workshop culture, we design balance into the way that a team works. This means looking at time spent working alone and time spent together, noticing where there may be intense periods of work and where there are opportunities for downtime. We start to address one of the core reasons for work-based well-being challenges – unsustainable ways of working. We do not need to restore our physical and mental health. Our workplaces are instead designed so that they don't drain us in the first place. Or even more radically, they become an environment that *gives* us more energy.

New ways of organizing and leading

A workshop culture can start to influence how we structure and lead our organizations:

- breaking down silos by creating more networked structures that bring talent together to collaborate from across departments and teams
- creating more iterative and frequent feedback and performance-review processes that emphasize collaboration over competition in their reward structures
- exploring alternative career progression routes for individuals based on their interests, strengths and the contribution they bring, rather than offering one single upwards route
- rethinking leadership styles that create a more inclusive and consistent experience for employees across an organization (even if that's just starting with how meetings are run!)
- looking at new ways of developing strategy in a responsive way that invite more voices in from across an organization so that resilience and adaptability are built in.

When we build more capacity for collaboration, we can reap tremendous results.

∞

This book started with some questions: what would it be like if you knew you and your colleagues could go to work, thrive and perform at your best? What if work was a place you went to develop and be fulfilled, not only professionally but also personally? What if you left work energized and excited, knowing that throughout your day you'd had moments of nourishing collaboration as well as the space to think and be creative?

A workplace culture can help businesses become more innovative by building better functioning organizations. It's also part of the wider conversation around how we make work better. Through exploring our personal routines, productivity methods and working styles, we become more aware of how we each grow and develop. We can make sure we do more of what we love, and use our strengths to transform our experience of work.

As so much of our work happens in teams, we must pay attention to how we work together. If we make work a place where we can thrive, it means we have more space and energy to have a positive impact on the people around us.

When we use the workplace as a true development ground for our personal growth, the knock-on effect is that this can help us become more fulfilled in our lives outside of work too. Our work is one of the biggest opportunities we have to come into contact with people different from ourselves and to learn how to collaborate effectively. It can be a springboard that makes us more curious about the world. We can build more empathy, appreciate diversity, and learn how to have better conversations and resolve conflict. Then those skills become available for us to use in any situation, including in our personal relationships, our communities and helping us towards a better society.

A final note: facilitators, we still need you!

A workshop culture is about spreading the skill of facilitation. So if everyone can facilitate, will we still need professional facilitators to run events like retreats and away days? Absolutely. There will always be a need for people to come together away from the workplace to participate in immersive experiences. When more people value facilitation and bring it into their skill set, professional facilitators can continue to advance the field.

Toolkit

Throughout the book, I've provided you with a range of practical 'REFLECTION' and 'TRY THIS' exercises. Combined, these make up your toolkit for preparing for, introducing and implementing a workshop culture. This is the list, in full with page numbers, so you can refer back to them easily.

Introduction

CHAPTER 1: The impact of the problem

CHAPTER 2: Why workshops are the solution

CHAPTER 3: Understanding workshop culture

Workshop Culture:
A Guide to Building Teams That
Thrive (summary)

Introduction

Workshop Culture: A Guide to Building Teams That Thrive comes from my experience of facilitating collaborative workshops and seeing how they help a team work better together. Through my work, I also discovered that when teams regularly run great workshops, it can have a positive impact on their wider culture. Workshops provide us with a snapshot into what a high-performing, engaged and collaborative team looks like. I've been exploring how teams could use these same tools to transform how they work for the long term, beyond a one-off event.

> Workshop culture = a team culture that uses the principles and practices of workshops and facilitation to encourage creativity and productivity, and to build the environment for effective collaboration.

This book breaks down the process, identifies the skills and mindset needed, and provides a five-pillar framework for building a workshop culture.

Part 1: Identifying the problem
Chapter 1: The impact of the problem

Modern organizations need collaboration, but they're not getting it right. This has more of a negative impact than we might think. As we spend so much time at work, and teamwork is a big part of this, the way we collaborate influences how we feel about our work. For example, meetings are a key feature of work life, but they are often poorly run. Bad meetings don't just waste time and money, they have an impact on engagement at work. Just by addressing this key aspect of our organizations, we can already go some way to improving culture.

Employees want more meaning and purpose in their work, and this can no longer be left to chance. Engagement affects productivity – a happy team environment is not mutually exclusive from a high-performance culture. Workshops are great examples of where we see great results *and* engaged teams. So what can we learn from this to improve our working environment?

Chapter 2: Why workshops are the solution

Workshops have many characteristics that we want to see in future-fit organizations, such as curiosity, learning and experimentation; open communication and visible progress; and responsiveness, emergence and iteration. For example, curiosity has been identified as a key contributor to innovation. Workshops help us get comfortable with the messy process of creativity – something we need if we want more innovation in our organizations. Workshops also ensure that people can speak up and share their ideas, which contributes to them feeling more valued.

A facilitator strives for psychological safety, diversity, healthy conflict, autonomy and transparency – again all characteristics of an environment that supports great collaboration. These are all elements that you will be designing for in a workshop culture. Start by assessing the extent to which these characteristics currently feature in your culture to explore how workshop principles can help your team to improve.

Part 2: Introducing workshop culture

Chapter 3: Understanding workshop culture

If you can remember what you felt in a really great workshop, you'll get a sense of what a workshop culture feels like. You're fully engaged; it feels buzzy and dynamic. You're more open and more connected to your colleagues. A workshop culture extends this feeling beyond the end of a workshop so that it becomes a natural part of work. This means workshops become more than a one-off event; where they no longer feel like they are the only place you can be creative. Instead you've learnt to bring more creativity into your everyday and use it to support productivity, rather than these two factors being at conflict with each other.

In addition, a workshop culture encourages teams to take an iterative approach to change and be intentional about the environment they want to create. We aren't expecting everything to happen spontaneously and all at once. Instead we use design principles to effect change gradually, and introduce regular workshops that build on each other. This means that change is more likely to stick.

Chapter 4: Leading a workshop culture

Introducing a workshop culture to your team is about more than running more workshops. It will also require a shift in perspective and the development of some key skills. Firstly, you will need a core belief in and a drive for *collaboration* and to build *facilitation* skills. Secondly, you will need to balance the needs of the *people* on your team and the needs of the *business*. Finally, you will need to complement the act of *thinking* about your culture with *doing* what it takes to make your ideas become reality. This needs strategic thinking, the ability to turn ideas to action, a design mindset and an understanding of behaviour change.

There will likely be some different feelings and emotions to work through as you transition towards a more facilitative approach in leading your team. If you've already had experience in preparing, facilitating and following-up workshops; you'll already have some of these transferable skills. If you haven't, the book digs into this in more detail.

Part 3: The framework

Chapter 5: Alignment – seeing the bigger picture

Each person on your team brings their own individual skills and perspective. Combine this with the work your team needs to do and the context you work within, and you have your unique team culture. This is all within a constantly changing and dynamic environment. So to transition towards a workshop culture, your team will also need to adapt their mindset and approach to the way they work together. They will need to be growth-mindset oriented, and truly believe that they can improve collaboration as a team. Again, it requires understanding how design, facilitation and behaviour change are a necessary part of the process.

To start off, you'll all need to take a step back to look at the bigger picture so that you can fully align around your vision and values. When you elevate your team in this way, to thinking at a higher level beyond their individual contribution, this empowers and engages them. It sets the tone for having better conversations about *how* you work together.

Chapter 6: Cohesion – self-awareness and connection

Cohesion on a team builds trust and supports collaboration. But to build a better connection with others, each team member needs a good level of self-awareness. The reflection activities required to do this are not normally seen as a part of work, so we need to create spaces for it if we want to build high-performing teams. This is more than personality tests. It also comes down to understanding our own working rhythms and productivity methods. When we build this understanding of ourselves, we can see how we show up and interact with others. This is the start of building mutual empathy, which breeds psychological safety and nurtures a more diverse environment.

Chapter 7: Communication – meetings and workshops

Bringing more facilitation into your regular meetings makes them more effective, and will also impact how your team works together. This becomes even more powerful when everyone has an insight into what it's like to facilitate great meetings and workshops. When everyone on a team learns facilitation skills, it helps them to both lead better sessions and build better communication skills.

Naturally, a facilitator learns how to manage group dynamics, support progress and encourage open dialogue. But there's also a duty for them to design meetings and workshops with a clear purpose so that they reach intended outcomes. When meetings are designed more purposefully, there will be distinct formats to support the different types of work you need to do. This contributes to a more effective and productive team culture.

Chapter 8: Design – designing ways of working

View your team culture as something that will always evolve. You will need to reassess, reset and refresh your ways of working depending on what is happening in your environment. While annual away days and team retreats are still valuable, they shouldn't be the only time you focus on 'team building'. Instead, think about how you build your team as you work together daily by creating rituals and routines that reflect your values.

Teams can design ways of working to optimize productivity, manage workloads and stay connected. Remote and hybrid teams can design how they use tech tools to support their work, when they need to come together and what they will do in those times, and what they will do when they are apart.

Chapter 9: Change – continuous improvement

Transforming our teams towards a workshop culture means adapting and undoing unproductive habits. Although this can be challenging, we can make it easier if we understand the mechanics of how we change our behaviour. By using our environment, creating micro-actions, building consistency, stacking habits and using nudges, we can gradually shift ourselves and our team towards the culture that we have envisaged. This will make the language of 'change' and continuous improvement become a regular conversation in our teams.

We can also support the process of change by providing coaching and by building a team culture roadmap with milestones so that we can measure progress and stay on track.

Conclusion

A workshop culture starts with transformation at the team level. But what could it look like when adopted across an entire organization? The flexibility and autonomy that a workshop culture creates brings more engagement. It provides an opportunity to attract talent, improve retention and create more diverse workplaces along with more sustainable and healthier ways of working. It can also influence how we structure and lead our organizations, breaking down silos, providing alternative career progression routes, creating more iterative performance-review processes and engaging a wider range of voices in strategy development.

Notes

Introduction

1. Behnam Tabrizi '75% of Cross-Functional Teams Are Dysfunctional', *Harvard Business Review* (23 June 2015). Available from: https://hbr.org/2015/06/75-of-cross-functional-teams-are-dysfunctional (accessed 10 June 2023).

Chapter 1

1. Deloitte 'Organisational Performance: It's a Team Sport (2019 Global Human Capital Trends)', Deloitte Insights (11 April 2019). Available from: www2.deloitte.com/us/en/insights/focus/human-capital-trends/2019/team-based-organization.html (accessed 10 June 2023).

2. Steven G. Rogelberg, Cliff Scott and Jim Kello 'The Science and Fiction of Meetings' in *MIT Sloan Management Review*, 48 (December), 18–21 (2007).

3. Doodle 'The Doodle State of Meetings Report 2019' in *Doodle 2019*. Available from: https://assets.ctfassets.net/p24lh3qexxeo/axrPjsBSD1bLp2HYEqoij/d2f08c2aaf5a6ed80ee53b5ad7631494/Meeting_Report_2019.pdf (accessed 10 June 2023).

4. Simone Kauffeld and Nale Lehmann-Willenbrock 'Meetings Matter: Effects of Work Group Communication on Organizational Success' *Small Group Research*, 43 (April), 130–158 (2012).

5. Kyle Benson 'The Magic Relationship Ratio, According to Science' The Gottman Institute. Available from: https://www.gottman.com/blog/the-magic-relationship-ratio-according-science (accessed 10 June 2023).

6. Joseph E. Mroz, Joseph A. Allen, Dana C. Verhoeven and Marissa L. Shuffler 'Do We Really Need Another Meeting? The Science of Workplace Meetings' in *Current Directions in Psychological Science* (October), 1–8 (2018).

7. 'APA Survey Finds Being Valued at Work Linked to Well-being and Performance' (2012). Available from: https://www.apa.org/news/press/releases/2012/03/well-being (accessed 11 June 2023).

8. Steven G. Rogelberg, Joseph A. Allen, Linda S. Hancock, Cliff Scott and Marissa Shuffler 'Employee Satisfaction with Meetings: A Contemporary Facet of Job Satisfaction' in *Human Resource Management,* 49 (2, March–April), 149–172 (2010).

9. Joseph A. Allen and Steven G. Rogelberg *Manager-Led Group Meetings: A Context for Promoting Employee Engagement* in *Group & Organization Management: An International Journal,* 38 (5), 543–569 (2013).

10. Gabriela Riccardi 'Does Your Team Need a Meeting Reset?' in *Quartz* (4 January 2023). Available from: https://qz.com/why-your-team-should-try-a-meeting-reset-1849949241 (accessed 10 June 2023).

11. Jim Harter 'Dismal Employee Engagement is a Sign of Global Mismanagement' in *Gallup* (20 December 2017). Available from: https://news.gallup.com/opinion/gallup/224012/dismal-employee-engagement-sign-global-mismanagement.aspx (accessed 10 June 2023).

12. James K. Harter, Frank L. Schmidt, and Theodore L. Hayes 'Business-Unit-Level Relationship Between Employee Satisfaction, Employee Engagement, and Business Outcomes: A Meta-Analysis' in *Journal of Applied Psychology,* 87 (2), 268–279 (2002).

13. Michael C. Bush 'This Is What Makes Employees Happy At Work' *TED/The Way We Work series.* Available from: www.youtube.com/watch?v=PYJ22-YYNW8 (accessed 10 June 2023).

14. Michael C. Bush 'This Is What Makes Employees Happy At Work' *TED/The Way We Work* series. Available from: www.youtube.com/watch?v=PYJ22-YYNW8 (accessed 10 June 2023).

15. Teresa Amabile and Steven Kramer *The Progress Principle: Using Small Wins to Ignite Joy, Engagement and Creativity at Work* (Harvard Business Review Press, 2011).

16. Shawn Achor, Andrew Reece, Gabriella Rosen Kellerman and Alexi Robichaux '9 Out of 10 People Are Willing to Earn Less Money to Do More Meaningful Work' in *Harvard Business Review* (6 November 2018). Available from: https://hbr.org/2018/11/9-out-of-10-people-are-willing-to-earn-less-money-to-do-more-meaningful-work (accessed 10 June 2023).

17. Joseph Fuller and William Kerr 'The Great Resignation Didn't Start with the Pandemic' in *Harvard Business Review* (23 March 2022). Available from: https://hbr.org/2022/03/the-great-resignation-didnt-start-with-the-pandemic (accessed 10 June 2023).

18. Elaine Pofeldt 'Are We Ready for a Workforce That Is 50% Freelance?' in *Forbes* (17 October 2017). Available from: www.forbes.com/sites/elainepofeldt/2017/10/17/are-we-ready-for-a-workforce-that-is-50-freelance/?sh=2dc95f243f82 (accessed 10 June 2023).

19. 'Rewriting the Rules: Building a Healthy Hybrid Workplace' in *The Economist* (2022). Available from: https://impact.economist.com/projects/rewriting-the-rules/pdfs/rewriting-the-rules-building-a-healthy-hybrid-workplace.pdf (accessed 10 June 2023).

20. Naina Dhingra, Andrew Samo, Bill Schaninger, and Matt Schrimper 'Help Your Employees Find Purpose – or Watch Them Leave' in *McKinsey* (5 April 2021). Available from: www.mckinsey.com/capabilities/people-and-organizational-performance/our-insights/help-your-employees-find-purpose-or-watch-them-leave (accessed 10 June 2023).

Chapter 2

1. Ben Wigert and Jennifer Robinson 'Fostering Creativity at Work: Do Your Managers Push or Crush Innovation?' in *Gallup* (19 December 2018). Available from: www.gallup.com/workplace/245498/fostering-creativity-work-managers-push-crush-innovation.aspx (accessed 10 June 2023).

2. Dave Gray, Sunni Brown and James Macanufo *Gamestorming: A Playbook for Innovators, Rulebreakers and Changemakers* (O'Reilly, 2010) p. 18.

3. Mordor Intelligence Research & Advisory 'Collaborative Whiteboard Software Market Size & Share Analysis – Growth Trends & Forecasts (2023–2028)' in *Mordor Intelligence* (June 2023). Available from: www.mordorintelligence.com/industry-reports/collaborative-whiteboard-software-market (accessed 21 July 2023).

4. Francesca Gino 'The Business Case for Curiosity' in *Harvard Business Review* (September–October), 48–57 (2018). Available from: https://hbr.org/2018/09/the-business-case-for-curiosity (accessed 10 June 2023).

5. 'Design Thinking Defined', *IDEO*. Available from: https://designthinking.ideo.com/ (accessed 10 June 2023).

6. Charles Duhigg 'What Google Learned from Its Quest to Build the Perfect Team' in *The New York Times Magazine* (25 February 2016). Available from: https://www.nytimes.com/2016/02/28/magazine/what-google-learned-from-its-quest-to-build-the-perfect-team.html (accessed 10 June 2023).

7. Amy Edmondson 'Psychological Safety and Learning Behavior in Work Teams' in *Administrative Science Quarterly*, 44 (2), 350–383 (1999).

8. David Rock and Heidi Grant 'Why Diverse Teams are Smarter' in *Harvard Business Review* (4 November 2016). Available from: https://hbr.org/2016/11/why-diverse-teams-are-smarter (accessed 11 June 2023).

9. 'Six Thinking Hats', The de Bono Group. Available from: www.debonogroup.com/services/core-programs/six-thinking-hats/ (accessed 10 June 2023).

10. Jake Knapp, John Zeratsky and Braden Kowitz *Sprint: How to Solve Big Problems and Test New Ideas in Just Five Days* (Penguin Random House, 2016) pp. 228–229.

11. Rebecca Johannsen and Paul J. Zak 'Autonomy Raises Productivity: An Experiment Measuring Neurophysiology' in *Frontiers in Psychology*, 11 (May), doi: 10.3389/fpsyg.2020.00963 (2023).

Chapter 3

1. Teresa M. Amabile 'How to Kill Creativity' in *Harvard Business Review* (September–October 1998). Available from: https://hbr.org/1998/09/how-to-kill-creativity (accessed 10 June 2023).

2. 'Group Dynamics' in *American Psychological Association* APA Dictionary of Psychology (2023). Available from: https://dictionary.apa.org/group-dynamics (accessed 10 June 2023).

3. Alex 'Sandy' Pentland 'The New Science of Building Great Teams' in *Harvard Business Review* (April 2012). Available from: https://hbr.org/2012/04/the-new-science-of-building-great-teams (accessed June 2023).

Chapter 4

1. Stephen Covey *The 7 Habits of Highly Effective People* (Simon & Schuster, 2013).

2. Teresa M. Amabile 'How to Kill Creativity' in *Harvard Business Review* (September–October 1998). Available from: https://hbr.org/1998/09/how-to-kill-creativity (accessed 10 June 2023).

3. Abraham Carmeli and Paul B. Paulus 'CEO Ideational Facilitation Leadership and Team Creativity: The Mediating Role of Knowledge Sharing' in *The Journal of Creative Behaviour*, 49 (1), 53–75 (2015).

4. Edgar H. Schein *Humble Inquiry: The Gentle Art of Asking Instead of Telling* (Berrett-Koehler, 2013) p. 2.

5. Robert Kabacoff 'Develop Strategic Thinkers Throughout Your Organization', *Harvard Business Review* (7 February 2014). Available from: https://hbr.org/2014/02/develop-strategic-thinkers-throughout-your-organization (accessed 10 June 2023).

6. Joan Meyers-Levy and Rui (Juliet) Zhu 'The Influence of Ceiling Height: The Effect of Priming on the Type of Processing That People Use' in *Journal of Consumer Research*, 34 (August) 174–186 (2007).

7. 'History of the Double Diamond' Design Council. Available from: www.designcouncil.org.uk/our-resources/the-double-diamond/history-of-the-double-diamond/ (accessed 10 June 2023).

8. Scott Belsky *Making Ideas Happen: Overcoming the Obstacles Between Vision and Reality* (Portfolio, 2010).

Chapter 5

1. Andre Martin and Vidula Bal 'The State of Teams', Center for Creative Leadership (2015). Available from: https://cclinnovation.org/wp-content/uploads/2020/03/stateofteams.pdf (accessed 19 July 2023).

2. Carol S. Dweck *Mindset: How You Can Fulfil Your Potential* (Robinson, 2012).

3. Daniel Pink *Drive: The Surprising Truth about What Motivates Us* (Canongate Books, 2011).

4. Daniel Pink *Drive: The Surprising Truth about What Motivates Us* (Canongate Books, 2011).

Chapter 6

1. Linda A. Hill, Greg Brandeau, Emily Truelove and Kent Line Back *Collective Genius: The Art and Practice of Leading Innovation* (Harvard Business Review Press, 2014) p. 28.

2. Center for Advanced Human Resource Studies *Getting to Know You: Self-Awareness Is Key for High-Performing, Adaptive Teams* (CAHRS Research Link No. 11, September 2010).

3. Tasha Eurich *Insight: How to Succeed by Seeing Yourself Clearly* (Macmillan, 2017).

4. Emma Goldberg 'The $2 Billion Question of Who You Are At Work' in *New York Times* (5 March 2023). Available from: www.nytimes.com/2023/03/05/business/remote-work-personality-tests.html (accessed 10 June 2023).

5. Emma Goldberg 'The $2 Billion Question of Who You Are At Work', in *New York Times* (5 March 2023). Available from: www.nytimes.com/2023/03/05/business/remote-work-personality-tests.html (accessed 10 June 2023).

6. Giada Di Stefano, Francesca Gino, Gary Pisano and Bradley Staats *Learning By Thinking: How Reflection Can Spur Progress Along the Learning Curve.* Accepted for publication on Management Science, Harvard Business School NOM Unit Working Paper No. 14-093 (6 February 2023).

7. HBS Communications 'Problem-Solving Techniques Take on New Twist' in *The Harvard Gazette* (15 August 2018). Available from: https://news.harvard.edu/gazette/story/2018/08/collaborate-on-complex-problems-but-only-intermittently/ (accessed 10 June 2023).

8. Rob Cross, Mike Benson, Jack Kostal and RJ Milnor 'Collaboration Overload is Sinking Productivity' in *Harvard Business Review* (7

September 2021). Available from: https://hbr.org/2021/09/collaboration-overload-is-sinking-productivity (accessed 11 June 2023).

9. Cal Newport *Deep Work: Rules For Focused Success in a Distracted World* (Piatkus, 2016) p. 3.

10. Teresa Amabile and Steven Kramer *The Progress Principle: Using Small Wins to Ignite Joy, Engagement and Creativity at Work* (Harvard Business Review Press, 2011).

11. Alison Jones *Exploratory Writing: Everyday Magic for Life and Work* (Practical Inspiration Publishing, 2023) p. 57.

12. Adam Bryant 'Want to Know Me? Just Read my User Manual' in *New York Times* (30 March 2013). Available from: www.nytimes.com/2013/03/31/business/questbacks-lead-strategist-on-his-user-manual.html (accessed 10 June 2023).

13. 'empathy' *Merriam-Webster.com*. Merriam-Webster (2023). Available from: www.merriam-webster.com/dictionary/empathy (accessed 9 June 2023).

14. Dave Gray 'Empathy Map' in *Gamestorming* (14 July 2017). Available from: https://gamestorming.com/empathy-mapping/ (accessed 10 June 2023).

Chapter 7

1. Atul Gawande *The Checklist Manifesto: How to Get Things Right* (Profile Books, 2011) p. 108.

2. M. Greer 'People's Performance Slows, Falters When Switching to a New Task' in *American Psychological Association*, 36 (4), (April 2005). Available from: www.apa.org/monitor/apr05/newtask (accessed 11 June 2023).

Chapter 8

1. Taylor Lorenz 'How Asana Built the Best Company Culture in Tech' in *Fast Company* (29 May 2017). Available from: www.fastcompany. com/3069240/how-asana-built-the-best-company-culture-in-tech (accessed 11 June 2023). Also see Justin Rosenstein's presentation for Lean Startup Week 2017 www.youtube.com/watch?v=o1LeIf2BteU (accessed 11 June 2023).

2. Ethan Mollick and Nancy Rothbard 'Mandatory Fun: Consent, Gamification and the Impact of Games at Work' in *The Wharton School Research Paper Series* (30 September 2014). Available from: SSRN: https:// ssrn.com/abstract=2277103 or http://dx.doi.org/10.2139/ssrn.2277103 (accessed 11 June 2023).

3. Kursat Ozenc, Ph.D. and Margaret Hagan, Ph.D. *Rituals for Work: 50 Ways to Create Engagement, Shared Purpose and a Culture That Can Adapt to Change* (Wiley, 2019).

4. Vinod Yadav 'An Introduction to Cognitive Load Theory' in *Cognitive Load: A Learning Teaching Perspective* (March), 30–45 (2023). Available from: www.researchgate.net/publication/369465946_An_Introduction_ to_Cognitive_Load_Theory (accessed 11 June 2023).

5. Vinod Yadav 'An Introduction to Cognitive Load Theory' in *Cognitive Load: A Learning Teaching Perspective* (March), 30–45 (2023). Available from: www.researchgate.net/publication/369465946_An_Introduction_ to_Cognitive_Load_Theory (accessed 11 June 2023).

6. Mihaly Csikszentmihalyi *Flow: The Psychology of Optimal Experience* (Harper and Row, 1990). Csikszentmihalyi published several books on 'Flow'. This is just one!

7. Steven Kotler 'Create a Work Environment That Fosters Flow' in *Harvard Business Review* (6 May 2014; updated 11 October 2019). Available from:

https://hbr.org/2014/05/create-a-work-environment-that-fosters-flow (accessed 11 June 2023).

8. Keith Sawyer 'Group Flow and Group Genius' in *The NAMTA Journal*, 40 (3), 29–52 (Summer 2015).

9. Keith Sawyer 'Group Flow and Group Genius' in *The NAMTA Journal*, 40 (3), 29–52 (Summer 2015).

10. Jef J.J. van den Hout, Orin C. Davis, and Bob Walrave 'The Application of Team Flow Theory' in *Flow Experience* (Springer, April 2016). Available from: https://doi.org/10.1007/978-3-319-28634-1_15 (accessed 11 June 2023).

11. Jef J.J. van den Hout, Orin C. Davis, and Bob Walrave 'The Application of Team Flow Theory' in *Flow Experience* (Springer, April 2016). Available from: https://doi.org/10.1007/978-3-319-28634-1_15 (accessed 11 June 2023).

12. Miro 'Asynchronous Work Report: What Knowledge Workers Want and What's Working', *Miro.com*. Available from: https://miro.com/blog/asynchronous-work-report/ (accessed 11 June 2023).

Chapter 9

1. Jennifer A. Chatman, David F. Caldwell, Charles A. O'Reilly and Bernadette Doerr 'Parsing Organizational Culture: How the Norm for Adaptability Influences the Relationship Between Culture Consensus and Financial Performance in High-Technology Firms' in *Journal of Organizational Behavior*, 35 (6), 785–808 (2014).

2. Ann M. Graybiel 'Habits, Rituals, and the Evaluative Brain' in *Annual Review of Neuroscience*, 31, 359–387 (2008).

3. Mark Muraven and Roy F. Baumeister 'Self-Regulation and Depletion of Limited Resources: Does Self-Control Resemble a Muscle?' in *Psychological Bulletin*, 126 (2), 247–259 (2000).

4. James Clear *Atomic Habits: An Easy and Proven Way to Build Good Habits and Break Bad Ones* (Penguin Random House, 2017) p. 85.

5. Maria Godoy and Sylvie Douglis 'Instead of New Year's Resolutions, Start and Stick with "Tiny Habits"', NPR. Available from: www.npr.org/2020/02/25/809256398/tiny-habits-are-the-key-to-behavioral-change (accessed 12 June 2023).

6. James Clear *Atomic Habits: An Easy and Proven Way to Build Good Habits and Break Bad Ones* (Penguin Random House, 2017) p. 196.

7. Charles Duhigg *Power of Habit: Why We Do What We Do and How to Change* (Random House Books, 2013) p. 35.

8. Wendy Wood *Good Habits, Bad Habits: The Science of Making Positive Changes That Stick* (Macmillan, 2019) p. 141.

9. Richard M. Ryan and Edward L. Deci 'Self-Determination Theory and the Facilitation of Intrinsic Motivation, Social Development, and Well-Being' in *American Psychologist*, 55 (1), 68–78 (2000).

10. Peter M. Gollwitzer 'Implementation Intentions' in *American Psychologist*, 54 (7), 493–503 (1999).

11. Lukas J. Thürmer, Frank Wieber and Peter M. Gollwitzer 'Strategic Self-Regulation in Groups: Collective Implementation Intentions Help Cooperate When Cooperation Is Called For' in *Frontiers in Psychology*, 11, Article 561388 (2020).

12. Thomas J. Delong 'Three Questions for Effective Feedback' in *Harvard Business Review* (4 August 2011). Available from: https://hbr.org/2011/08/three-questions-for-effective-feedback (accessed 10 June 2023).

13. 'Impact Effort Matrix' *ASQ.org*. Available from: https://asq.org/quality-resources/impact-effort-matrix (accessed 10 June 2023).

Acknowledgements

Each phase of the book writing process has its own triumphs and challenges, and I've had tremendous support and encouragement from many people at different stages of the journey.

Firstly, thank you to all the writers, thinkers, academics, experts, and practitioners who have inspired me – during my MA studies and throughout my career to date – many of whom I've referenced in the book. Thank you to all my clients, collaborators, colleagues and conversation partners who have provided a space for me to further hone my ideas, methodology and approach.

The idea for this book was brought to life in my second attempt of Alison Jones's powerful ten-day business book proposal challenge back in 2018. Thank you for believing in it from the outset, and for your patience while I prepared to write it!

Thank you to those who generously gave their time for interviews – Emma Robertson, Hazel Swayne, Kai Haley, Kirk de Vallis, Krys Burnette, Sam Hoey and Sara Elnusairi. Although those initial conversations didn't make it into this final version, they helped to shape my thinking.

Huge thanks to Jonas Altman for reading my messy, early thoughts before I even got to first draft and to Jo Bennett for helping me to refine the core message and re-work the structure so that it made perfect sense. To Neil Vass (beta-reader extraordinaire!) and chapter reviewers – Aleksandra Melnikova, Alexander Baxevanis, Alison Tansey, Cheryl Savage, Christina Langdon, David Hughes, Dominique Exmann, Gareth Marlow, Holly Davis, Justine Paul, Lauren Kaplan, Lorna Murphy, R.M. Michaële Antoine and Sonja Stojanović Gajić – I deeply appreciate your time, attention and feedback.

I wrote most of this book while using Groove, a digital co-working and accountability app. Thank you to everyone I 'grooved' with for cheering me on.

Thank you to Gabija Jankauskaite for the front cover design, illustrations and general creative insight and direction. You have a true talent! Thank you to Elisa Duriavig for your support in those especially crunchy times when book-writing was naturally competing with client work.

Many thanks to Dave Gray for the use of the empathy map canvas, to the Design Council for use of the Double Diamond, and to Dan Porter and his team at Scriberia for the wonderful bespoke sketchnote.

Eternal gratitude to Alex Osterwalder for writing a fantastic foreword. Your encouragement and mentorship over the years, plus observing and learning from the Strategyzer workshops have been integral to my realising the potential of workshop culture.

Thanks to the team at Practical Inspiration, Shell, Michelle and Francis; Katherine Hartle, development editor, for helping me to refine my writing; and Tristen Bakker, copyeditor for those final tweaks. Erin Wiegand at Newgen – you are the most patient production editor, ever. Thank you all for your grace and optimism while dealing with this recovering perfectionist!

And finally, thank you to my supportive family, and my parents, Icilda Austrie and Ricardo Coward, for, well, everything.

About the Author

Alison Coward is the founder of Bracket, a team culture consultancy that partners with ambitious, forward-thinking organizations to help them build high-performing teams. She is a workshop facilitator, consultant, and speaker with clients ranging across the creative, media, technology and digital sectors. Alison is passionate about finding the balance between creativity, productivity and collaboration so that teams can thrive and do their best work together.

Alison has been working in, leading and facilitating creative teams since early in her career and has an MA in Enterprise Management for the Creative Arts from University of the Arts London. She has delivered guest lectures at universities, workshops at conferences and keynote talks on the topics of collaboration and team culture in the UK, across Europe and in the US. Her first book, *A Pocket Guide to Effective Workshops*, was published in 2015.

To find out more, visit www.bracketcreative.co.uk.

Index

A quick word from Practical Inspiration Publishing...

We hope you found this book both practical and inspiring – that's what we aim for with every book we publish.

We publish titles on topics ranging from leadership, entrepreneurship, HR and marketing to self-development and wellbeing.

Find details of all our books at: www.practicalinspiration.com

 Did you know...

We can offer discounts on bulk sales of all our titles – ideal if you want to use them for training purposes, corporate giveaways or simply because you feel these ideas deserve to be shared with your network.

We can even produce bespoke versions of our books, for example with your organization's logo and/or a tailored foreword.

To discuss further, contact us on info@practicalinspiration.com.

 **Got an idea for a business book?**

We may be able to help. Find out more about publishing in partnership with us at: bit.ly/PIpublishing.

Follow us on social media...

 @PIPTalking

 @pip_talking

 @practicalinspiration

 @piptalking

in Practical Inspiration Publishing

Printed in the USA
CPSIA information can be obtained
at www.ICGtesting.com
JSHW011056160124
55462JS00012B/92

9 781788 604710